The Rituals

of

Mummification

Joseph D. Reich

© 2016 by Joseph D. Reich
Book design © 2016 by Sagging Meniscus Press

All Rights Reserved.

Printed in the United States of America.
Set in Williams Caslon Text with LaTeX.

ISBN: 978-1-944697-20-4 (paperback)
ISBN: 978-1-944697-19-8 (ebook)
Library of Congress Control Number: 2016953613

Sagging Meniscus Press
web: http://www.saggingmeniscus.com/
email: info@saggingmeniscus.com

For not just the '69 & '73 championship Knicks but everyone else at the old Garden, which included Red Holtzman & the scalpers & drug dealers & vendors who sold cold hotdogs & warm beer

The Rituals of Mummification

Contents

The Hospitality Business   3

Hoard-a-culture   17

Home Economics   81

A Hx Of Stream Of Consciousness   93

The Rituals of Mummification

The Hospitality Business

passing time

"Over the river and I'll see you in the funnies!"

—Anonymous

The Rituals of Mummification

A bum gets picked up off the curb
and much to the surprise of the merchant
the first words he enthusiastically blurts—
"Top o' the morning to ya!"

3:30

whenever my shift used to begin
to calm myself down i would take
long solemn strolls up and down
the boardwalk and check out
the stray dogs and blind men
and old men roaming like sleep
walkers with transistors pasted
to their ears and black boys like
acrobats of pure freedom doing
backflips off the scorching stairs

4:15

stare bleary-eyed through big blazing windows
after having polished down the luggage carts
having noticed the man in the hot ice truck
is passed-out with his motor still running
like some mafioso bludgeoned outside
the front entrance could be dusk
or dawn really doesn't matter

The Hospitality Business

5:30

the weather is everything which creeps past your window

5:36

the doorman naturally changes his whistle
from metal to wood at the change of seasons

5:37

secretaries really lonely sailors are seagulls
searching for leftovers and this is the whole
lost and desperate 'hustle & bustle' life-cycle
not sure if it's the beat and rhythm of her heels
or the clip-clop of the mounted police on the curb

5:45

the sepia tugs and ferries come
putt-putt putting into harbor some
for commuting some for commerce
while the property when it got sold
not too long ago seems like ages ago
and turned from residential to hotel
some just (or couldn't or wouldn't)
refused to go like that industrious
old man from the diamond district
who had spent a whole existence

The Rituals of Mummification

and refused to be told when to exit
and sweeps in every twilight
and every season looking pale
and polluted as if the lingering
light of a once great radiant
and distant city remains in him
and like everything else, faded
(the hyperbole of what it seems
or looks like or feels to be forgotten)
and picks up the paper from the front
desk with the same ashen complexion
and makes a little small talk with
the concierge and even the guests
humble and honest yet can't help
but to present as excruciatingly
lonesome and distressed from
fate and circumstance also has
no choice but to be a bit critical
and judgmental as if left behind
for no particular reason by a
whole generation and vanishes
to his solitary destination
disappearing up the elevator

5:56

a marquee put up in the lobby for the cosmetologist convention

The Hospitality Business

6:02

in the background of the elevator you can faintly hear
the late-great george harrison crooning–'i really want
to see you lord...i really want to feel you lord...but
it takes so long...hare krishna...krishna...krishna...'
while bleached blondes just out of the university
completely oblivious and driven are studying
for their pharmaceutical tests (bio-tech, one
of the highest paying fields and up and coming
industries in america) the scientific and generic
names for the med; which one used to placate
a contained part of the brain; which one brings
about a certain equilibrium and complete
contentment for chemical imbalance or
angry outbursts and swings of emotion
(no longer *shuffling off to buffalo* against
their own will and volition) later on they
will get completely loud and obnoxious
blasted off banana daiquiris, and just like
their fragile 'behavior' and insecure 'character'
go into denial play possum and forget what happened

6:03

your best friend's father had a breakdown.
used to be real successful and the lawyer
for the stones; last we saw of him, just
saw him wandering around the suburbs
in his long shaggy beard with his long

The Rituals of Mummification

shaggy dog. we always wondered what
had happened and i always waved at him
hoping he'd somehow remember me (as
felt a heck of a lot of sympathy) and spent
the rest of his days listening to the beatles
just fading away in his sunroom; seemed like a
fine retirement, escape from reality and way to go

6:15

each and every evening like clockwork the same strange half-crazed tradition
of some night-auditor being chased down the sidewalk by some madman
wielding a machete then straightens his collar and his facial expressions
and vanishes up the elevator pretending like nothing had happened

he has the reputation for being a bit aloof and arrogant

as evidenced when situation brought to attention becomes a part
of his denial a part of the riddle a part of the punch line as well

6:32

i like the busloads of germans
and the busloads of asians
as they don't speak the
language and keep their
distance trying to make
the greatest connection
and most curious about
the culture we live in

The Hospitality Business

earnest expressions
seeming the most
satisfied and
contented

in the morning they leave their bags outside
the door and you get five dollars for each one

7:00

in the lounge the ventriloquist gets into a screaming match with his dummy
and grabs him by the hair and starts swinging him around and banging
his head against the stage; limbs go flying all over the place leaving
the audience in utter shock and awe; never seen anything like this
before and chokes the last of his look-a-like pal, then starts slowly
mouthing the words with a sarcastic drawl. suddenly someone from
the audience leaps up and hollers–"hey! why don't you try picking on

someone your own size!" he drops to his knees and starts
banging his skull against the stage. they bring in the lounge
singer on wheels all decked-out in a faux white boy afro and
out-of-date sequins like the pope-mobile coyly winking at them
or when they have to put the fast food workers behind the bullet
proof glass of *white castle* at curfew and gang members go flying
through the glass windows on queens boulevard having revelations

they all wake up numb experiencing something of a perverse
psychological phenomenon of a rebirth feeling like new men

The Rituals of Mummification

7:30

sisters borrowing vibrators from each other
(perhaps after one's broken, feeling broken)
both highly-intelligent and attractive and what
anxiety and the big city will do to you; one a doctor
and the other a social worker with so few really good men
out there, like the remains of 'the madonna/whore complex'
having given so much of themselves and been generous and now needing
so much more which is natural and instinctive and romantic and primitive

7:45

mean and nasty, stingy and sexless, aristocratic women
sneak past young couples patiently waiting in the vestibule

for taxis whose exclusivity and manners
is having absolutely no manners at all.

real sophistication is having tact and taste, knowing when to be subtle.
their husbands have all turned them into widows in one form or another

8:45

they do a group mailing of glossy brochures
showing a very sociopathic mathematician
in henry kissinger glasses sitting contented
in the cozy lounge gazing out to the lit-up
city after having just chopped up one of his
mistresses into a million pieces and ecstatic
family with pasted-on smiles sliding down

The Hospitality Business

the waterslide like an accordion; one of
those milfs stepping out of the pool...

11:45

the stud elevator repairmen and humble male dancer
show up with their equipment at all hours of the night

idiots from the pharmaceutical convention and loud
drunken middle-aged women have worn them all out

things always confused by role-reversals
or who's truly out there paying their dues

without the whole schmooze and
sincerely trying to make a living

12:02

some of them even have secret code names
like pornographic undercover kings and queens
to keep their loved ones back home off the trail.

one wonders where the suburbs begin and wildlife ends?
real true life and play pretend? in the morning they'll
come off the elevator as if nothing happened

you feel slightly nauseous in just feeling
too close to them like some relationship
you know should have ended staying
together merely for convenience
or the most vulgar of reasons

The Rituals of Mummification

12:14

every time you are called in there
when they are not there based on
some complaint or another to replace
a sheet or towel or pillow or light bulb
or even whole mattress because claim
"bedbugs" you feel like something
of a paranoid perverted criminal mad
scientist or deranged detective dusting
for fingerprints of lost and lonesome
souls trying to piece together evidence
of empty existences loveless marriages
tragic losses or worst of all someone
who just appears eternally stranded
as just never found the right soul mate
for whatever 'ridiculous' existential reason
drained from the pain of living…
mistaken identities, misunderstood
and underestimated; the remains of
all things misinterpreted and missing
like one of those tiny dishes of invisible ink
suddenly spilled all over them and sent them
against their own will and volition to a place
where they will instantly be forgotten for no
particular reason just the suffering of living

The Hospitality Business

12:25

with patterns and symptoms of guests
you find indifference (to try and impress)
not that particularly impressive but those of
compassion and spirit the ones who really made it

1:45

insurance salesmen from the midwest
what they like to refer to as "family men" try to sneak
in drag queens at all hours of the night from the meat market

the front desk supervisor who has been betrayed
by his wife and gone lesbian engages in a power-
struggle with them and hollers—"this is a family run!"

2:01

security wanders the halls
with those old time nostalgic
exhibitionist coats acting like
a cross between clint eastwood
and inspector clouseau with
napoleonic complexes

2:15

handsome greek from the corner diner
shows up with a gyro without sauce
french fries and an extra-dill pickle

The Rituals of Mummification

4:45

the doorman wakes up in the bellman's closet

4:51

communication log reads—
"bedbugs, ghosts"

5:02

everyone seems as fragile as glass animals
trying to hide their lost shattered souls

how in configuration, function and form, you figure out
the female is a semi-colon and male dangling participle

6:54

snapshots of sexual-intercourse (slide presentation)
linear and non-linear from stagnant to state of flux
where time stands still but also feels for the first
time 'moves right along' from the first kiss
and caress to the final climax of pleasure
of opening each other up and yes literally
becoming new specimens with no unnecessary
need for identity, playing roles, or function and form

The Hospitality Business

7:05

dresser drawers with playing cards
and tapes on 'how to make a killing
in the market,' xanex, souvenir snow globes
and panties with stained period blood in them

7:45

the pretty puerto rican housekeeping staff
show up as always (bright and early) giggling
better than any rising sun or sidewalk hosed down

8:05

the timekeeper sits outside inside of his tiny little booth
keeping an eye on everything out there and everything
within like one of those tow bridge operators
always missing as i guess he's union

8:36

a note on the door knob left for the overnight
guests tells them "thank you for your service"
and that the hotel has changed management

The Rituals of Mummification

8:41

bills slipped under doors by that soulful
and solitary bellman during his graveyard
like some denouement to an absurd drama
reminding them to put their mediocre and
made-to-fit disguises back on; to hit the road
and play the same unconvincing higher-than-holy
roles their family and corporation (pretty much
interchangeable) is expecting from them of quasi-
normal, see-through and pathetic, not even close

9:45

with his tips from the night before the doorman
will pick up those eggs and hashbrowns to die for
made by that one-armed veteran at that grill in the station
at the last stop in coney island; knock it all down with a cold
one and read the sports and weather with the rhythmic hypnotic echo
of the self-soothing surf from the distant ocean pounding his window
and in the instant or during this routine and ritual able to forget it all.

A bum gets picked up off the curb
and much to the surprise of the merchant
the first words he enthusiastically blurts—
"Top o' the morning to ya!"

Hoard-a-culture

on the making of aphorisms and noir

"I've been around that trashy behavior all my life.
I'm getting plenty tired of putting up with it..."

—The Last Picture Show

The Rituals of Mummification

1

you know how they got like all these scientific
medical names for anti-anxiety meds or painkillers?
well—i think they should have one for that generic
brand of human who try to steal everything from you

a thief's intuition is far better
than any honest man i ever knew…

2

definitions derive from very concrete and descriptive patterns
like the core nucleus and functioning of the atom or all the criteria
that make up a personality disorder and you go wow that's exactly it

3

you can compare forms and sensations and phenomenons
(even sensibilities which i guess we're often guilty of)
and i suppose you'd get reality but not really
like all those elements and things
which causes psychosomatic to be

4

it is 'nauseating' (and the sensation is very real)
when you consider how willing and with what vigor
and stubborn conviction (will even go so far as delusion)

Hoard-a-culture

people stick to their roles in a family system or even the
dysfunctional family unit and through their rigid thought
patterns and ways of coping and surviving could never
ever consider others beliefs or points-of-view as literally
and proverbially 'scared to death' and would instantly
shatter their very fragile identities and what they
have worked so hard to pathetically establish

5

if you grew up in the weird and wealthy workaholic suburbs
in the illusion of existence on the outskirts of being and reality
you pretty much were raised in a film-noir with the parents
never around and got acquainted with things you shouldn't
of; brooding way too long in large luxuriant rooms of turn
of the century furniture; the very intricate ornate detail
and ribald tales from the wallpaper where it all began
and ended and how they just tried to make it continue
as if there was never ever any pain or suffering in this
soft pastel flute-blowing courting and seductive existence;
your gardener who became your best friend and confidante;
your connections (when you were at a loss...) that gentle giant
black man who waxed the foyer and would simply slowly spin
round and round and round, nodding-out on heroin; the geometric
holy lonely shapes of the trees and lawns and brooks outside your
window growing larger and larger by the second in liberating rainfall

The Rituals of Mummification

6

how you used to just wish to be one of those souvenir conch shells
picked up from some souvenir gift shop in one of those caribbean
islands when the caribbean was still the caribbean and the holiday
inn was still the holiday inn by some diplomat's daughter who in fact
had actually seduced all the natives and literally made them do back
flips for her along the ocean and when she got home took that souvenir
conch shell like some sort of trophy or award and put it up all safe
and secure on one of those mantles somewhere between pictures of
a smiling psychotic family with all their secrets and craziness and
petty power-struggles and those perfect hardcover collections of the
classics like *winesburg, ohio* and *main street* and *bartelby the scrivener*
or like lincoln or churchill's diaries or 'new york times book of the
month club' and whenever you felt completely out of it and losing
it and wasn't going to make it from all the guilt and peer pressure
and unrealistic expectations of one of those fucked-up fictional
suburbs so far from any true sense of belief or baseline of reality
spending a whole youth not being able to stay out of trouble just
picking up that souvenir conch shell and putting it straight-up
against your ear and pavlovian-like or like some child plunked
for hours on his *radioflyer* horse hypnotically going into some
primordial trance still hearing all that sweet self-soothing babble
eternal echo of the ancient ocean which always instantly seemed
to put it all in perspective and provide an instant panacea heading back
to own private intimate and affectionate future arrested stage of development

Hoard-a-culture

7

my life & times as a silent home movie…
from the action & adventure of silent home movies
to weekends of *tarzan king of the jungle* to the brilliance
of *abbot & costello* to the skinned knees and scars of the
mud & blood of schoolyards to not being able to keep myself
out of trouble; the silent clown of detention hall and keeping it
all in; a tragic romantic, devastated and deflated at the school dance
deep-down inside knowing what a fool she is to go out with a fool like him

8

growing up out there felt like being a delinquent
against your own will and volition and taking
a gopher job during the summer at that stock
firm when they first started putting up those
business parks in the middle of nowhere
and having to follow the boss's wife to like
pick up his golf clubs and the whole time
giving me these lost and lonely longing
eyes not knowing why (mrs. robinson
you're not my type) and thought even
if she committed suicide with her guts
and insides splattered all over the place
would it really make much of a difference
still checking me out and trying to find their
outdated split-level stuck somewhere out there in
the middle of missing-in-action look-alike suburbs

The Rituals of Mummification

9

everything we deflected in childhood
was the stuff which held the most meaning
what we didn't want them to know anything…

very similar to the derivation
and dynamic of the natural and necessary
use and formation and functioning of language

10

premonitions & prophecies & dreams & fantasies & sixth senses
& past tenses & future tenses i guess has a little something to do
with the subconscious but in most ways just doesn't & deeper
& more shallow if you got a little experience in this world &
not being able to keep yourself out of trouble for all the right
reasons to know they're all just a bunch of fuckin blowhards
slut seductresses & false witnesses & not so innocent bystanders

never put your trust or faith in one of those phony
kiss asses or those bent on being driven & successes

11

last night like a miracle i had one of those
good dreams and all the pretty and gorgeous
and sophisticated girls and ladies were coming
onto me in new york city some even came back
to say they were sorry and hug me (and redeem)

Hoard-a-culture

which turned them into classic beauties o what
a sense of freedom (and relief) and being and
belonging! even in the labyrinths of old time
mahogany plush hotels and chinatown corner
shootouts where i picked up roses and took
those long endless strolls you take with some
newfound lover you feel like you've known
forever where you tell her your life story (and she
tells you hers) and get absolutely everything off
your chest and feel like this blissful and brilliant
emptiness (of a weightless levitating essence)
in effect (having nothing to do with effect and
the core nucleus of the innocent glowing soul)
is the true-blue lost & found ladder of success

12

in my opinion 'the bewitching hour'
has absolutely nothing to do with the child
but really started somewhere around puberty
and went all the way to 'later-adulthood' and
whose gloom & doom gradual darkness build-up
outside your window became a nihilistic trigger
to all of tomorrow's responsibilities and expectations
and anxieties and long-term future of fate and mortality

The Rituals of Mummification

13

how to read dostoevsky beneath mirrored ceilings
and not make something of yourself with mothballs
streaming out of pristine shag rug closets and all
those gorgeous cousins from weddings and bar-
mitzvahs turned to dope addicts in those high
rise doorman condos in the upper east side
where like some sci-fi movie no one really
lived existed or resided right around the
empty promenade of the united nations
and your best friends fathers all turned
to bachelors in the burnout days of disco
(always some rumor of some sort of marriage
infidelity and cheating and betrayal and them
feeling completely humiliated and a stigma
and internalizing even though they obviously
had absolutely nothing to do with it) and fated
to now become eternal commuters back and
forth between grand central and the suburbs

everything strangely somehow becoming a trigger
to the existential nothingness of being and reality

mandated psychiatrists and anger management…

Hoard-a-culture

14

like some cross between onset tourette's
and nonstop harassment constant bullshit
jewish guilt the trick was to say whatever
the fuck you wanted to say in whatever
fucken language you wanted to say it
and letting it all come out straight-up
however you felt it self-help advice
given from the new york time's bestseller
paperback by that yippie jerry ruben and
ironically he ended-up making millions
and his buddy abbie hoffman taking
his life never able to quite fit in
or feel a part of things or sense
of belonging or community with
that soulless breed of greedy yuppie

15

all seemed to end with the assassination
of john lennon and you just sitting there
dazed and numb and dead to the world
staring through the windshield with muted
tears running down your profile bleary-eyed
getting gas at the gas station in darkening dusk
believing at that exact moment myself turning off

The Rituals of Mummification

16

depression (or that numb feeling) is not always exactly
what it seems but the exacerbation of certain anxieties,
uncontrollable stressors and circumstances (and the
constant repetition and vicious cycle of people's poor
character and behavior, which often may lead either to
hostility or brooding or fixation of reality-based paranoia)
and emotional and spiritual triggers from previous realities

17

why is it often when things seem to be going pretty damn well
for you…remember all the way back to days of grade school
people will say some of the stupidest shit about you (as if you
were even asking?) or from a contrary point-of-view when you
are down-in-the-dumps give you the most lame and mundane
unrealistic neutral piece of advice (again as if were even asking?)
as both exchanges ironically just making you feel the exact same
feelings of so damn alone or conclusions about the nature of man

man, looking back at those bittersweet years
of later-adolescence and pubescence was such
brainwash and bullshit and shallow and superficial
as if the prom/porn queen really was like some
prostitute with all her connections and favoritism
(and how strange it is to brood and ruminate on that
term 'popular') treating everyone like a possession
and became a tradition or some routine and ritual
to be deferential or honored to be in her presence

Hoard-a-culture

as you learn
a little later
on it's
all about
presence
or lack
there of
hold-up in
the truckee
river just out
side reno
not no
wing
a living
breathing
soul below
all those used car lots
& schmucks on signs
running for senators
& some neon cross
on top of the hill
which goes
on in the
tick-tock
dusk
drifting
home
past dog
obedience
& alcoholics

The Rituals of Mummification

anon en masse
to a lonesome
room with a
ceiling fan
which just
makes the
air warmer
& strangle
the hell
out of
you
&
wish
you
had
1, 2, 3
packets
of sugar
to add
to your
un sweet
& kool
aid to
guzzle
down
with
your
louise
l'amour
& all

Hoard-a-culture

those
other
paper
backs
you
got
for
your
done
ate it
blood
not
having
a single
person
to write
a post
card
too
witchin
essence
in truth
makes
it all that
much more
surreal & blue
messin' with
your mortality
messin' with
your moods

The Rituals of Mummification

& yer the
unsolved
murder
with no
one to
turn to
a solitary
stranger
simply
looking
to be
loved
& a
proved
yet viewed
as suspicious
by those
who don't
know
them
selves
but
who's
the real
criminal
pulling
you
into
their
hell

Hoard-a-culture

    & stare
out thee
starry-
eyed
eternal
farewell
bus window
in a plume
of desert
dust ex-
purring
the lost
jigsaw
pieces
of the
united
states
of america
on-the-run
bleary-eyed
bummed
reborn
in the holy
hush from
midnight
to the
holy light
of dawn
hope
fully

The Rituals of Mummification

they
kept
your
easy
chair
for you
in your
lower
east
side
guard
den...

no wonder one turns towards arrested stages
of development or even for that matter your
deathbed and imagine such images of it just
being some clown doing those twisty balloons
of animals and kids with leftover condiments
of ketchup and mustard or chocolate smudged
all over their face jumping up and down before
you reach the pearly gates, maybe grand kids
guessing that's an elephant! dog! goat! a ghost!
meryl steubing, doc, gopher from "the love boat"
at your window, isaac the cool bartender doing that
cool brother move right before you enter the big fade

Hoard-a-culture

18

it is crazy the things we fall in love with
and the things we fall out of love with
as in looking back pretty much
was the exact same thing

19

looking back at my youth & childhood
it seemed like a series of retorts & quick
one-liners spending my after-school hours
in detention hall walking the halls with a heart
of gold & scrub brush & pail of suds not giving
a fuck 'cuz she was the one who was in
the wrong ode to my soulless typewriting
teacher developing a case of the kleptomania
yet something of a misguided thoughtful robin
hood giving them out as gifts to my family for pass
over even the hallmark cards for eight straight nights

20

my delinquent friend and i diligently joining the track team
really believing we'd make something of ourselves but after
about one day of practice taking off from the squad while
staggering through town and ducking into the supermarket
to rip-off a whole case of halloween cupcakes sharing them
down by the train tracks when the rush hour trains came

The Rituals of Mummification

rushing in from grand central somehow making it back
to the fields of dusk and taking off not really feeling an
ounce of guilt independent self-reliant and autonomous
(i guess deep-down inside making names for ourselves)

21

the common characteristics of the lifelong criminal
(who rarely cares about 'redeemable' and clinically
'narcissistic' and 'sociopathic' and 'sadistic' on a
white-collar level) which are the true-blue 'contra-
dictions' between human character and behavior
without showing any sense of remorse or contrition
runs through almost 'practically' every politician.
in every successful politician is a little megalomania…

22

one wonders about the infamous "board of trustees"
and what inspired and motivated them to have the
need to become a member of the board of trustees
as often simply a front (and overcompensation) for
deep-seated and profound guilt and conflict they
care (or don't even care) to come to terms with
and some really fucked-up shit they actually did
with absolutely no remorse or contrition to beloved
members of their own family (they were supposed to
'support' and cared more so about becoming these self-
centered and single-minded 'successful schmucks') and

perhaps in one fell swoop this new trophy and award will
provide them an instant raw sense of forgiveness and how they
are viewed by their peers and family and community alike most
likely their 'reputation' becoming these self-proclaimed or self-
appointed martyrs or esteemed members of the board of trustees
once again having all the control and pathetically playing the role
of moral and ethical judges or some ridiculous role model of 'sorts'

23

we can talk about
lincoln & kennedy
fdr & even his rough
rider cousin theodore
but how quick we are
to forget all those young
bucks who were the true-blue
ones who actually bit the bullet
bit the dust and built-up and
sacrificed their skin & bones
in damp fall foliage folklore
for the growth & development
of this great nation and whose
spirits still literally linger when
you take those road trips down
over mason-dixon into the deep
sweet smelling stamen magnolia
of muddy twisting swamp lagoon
river walt whitman known to them

The Rituals of Mummification

as something of an old holy white-
bearded sainted visiting nurse caring
& compassionate & listened to them
& really & sincerely gave a damn
the life & times of the paper boy
bernard baruch when he made
his first million…

24

consider all those fogs and mists under the bridge
as much as those which swallow and engulf and
eat them up and everything over it which will
eventually feather and sprinkle all those little
lost leftover eccentric towns and historic hamlets
hugging the cobblestone ground along the hudson
allowing them to grow and develop their own
reputation and personality and character and
sensibility and aesthetic during the multi-colored
maddening seasons with all those secret blasts
of foghorn like some beloved stepsister tapping
your startled shoulder and had no other choice
(becoming a whole other type of free will and
volition) but to make a companion and let in
and welcome right through the draft of sleepy
hollow lattices and keyholes and chimneys
and radiators when you were down in the dumps
and desperate and without you even knowing it
bringing about a rebirth and forgotten lingering

Hoard-a-culture

spirit from the sudden internal blast and bellow
at its deepest and most hollow core to the periphery
of its remaining rippling echo like some welcoming
criminal just as lonesome as yourself sneaking
through your window always wondering and
trying to figure out exactly where it came from.
somewhere around dawn you'd creep naked across
the chill floors of your long-lost lover in the soulful
shadows and shelter of the brilliant blazing leaves
of autumn beneath the awakening still silhouetted
spires and steeples which seemed like the only path
to heaven to check for leftovers in the refrigerator…

25

an epic hx of america in diorama form made-up of
old *pro-ked* sneaker boxes this time not leaving out
the vast variety of colorful indian tribes, all those wild
rivers and their soulful sister tributaries, the slave trade
and from what southern state they took off from and what
specific countries in africa they stole from, reconstruction,
chinese internment, the creation of vegas, the creation of
the 5 new york crime families, the philadelphia mob, the
influence of vaudeville and yiddish theater, consider charlie
chaplin, the bowery boys, and d.w. griffith, don't leave out later
the self-destructive rebels james dean, marlon brando, montgomery
cliff and those unsung unknown b-film film-noir monster martian
invaders from outer-space who only made it to the drive-in theaters,
when they started putting up *mcdonalds* and *kentucky fried chicken*

The Rituals of Mummification

and *friendly's* food stands when fribbles used to be called awful-awfuls,
presidential assassinations (never ever quite collectively psychologically
or spiritually recovering) the drug trade and influx of cocaine and heroin

26

why does everything which at once seemed
or presented as being so avant-garde and bohemian
eventually turn out somewhere down the line (after you
see through all the masks and remove all the disguises)
like just another whining advertisement slave to the system
as if it were really cool and hip to be of indifference
(almost turning oneself into a product of nepotism)
really daddy's little girl with connections or a
starving artist who can afford to be starving
turning anguish into an advertisement?

interesting when you get to really know them
are as guilty and full of moral contradictions
(driven and self-interested) as the people
they are supposedly rebelling against

27

all these require-
meant to learn
a second lane
widget all thee
mandated and

Hoard-a-culture

prerequisites
to become
a more
well-
rounded
individual
you god
duh be
kidding
& they call
this a higher
education?
well how
about just
once giving
us the free
will &
volition
to become
hour own people
& build up our
hearts & souls
& imagination
without all this
bullshit interference
from big brother
policy maker
only makes
me repress
more and

The Rituals of Mummification

become
more
re
sent
full and
reactive
and on
the run

28

so you got this
chump trump
the orange-faced
grownup oompa-
loompa who
supposedly
went to the wharton
school of business
at university of
pennsylvania
you got baby
bush who looks
and sounds like
elmer fudd who
went to yale
in new haven
connecticut
you got the

Hoard-a-culture

youngest
kennedy
who got
caught
cheating
on his
exams
at have-id
so tell me
how do
you figure
really is
the criteria
and standards
for higher
education
in america?

29

always got so much more when i left the museum
doors (and those long dim halls to the sudden shaft
of winter's sun) and that thick scent of hot pretzels
socked me right in the jaw and rope-a-dope down
the heart & soul than anything in those long boring
and laborious tours 'leaving so much to be desired'

The Rituals of Mummification

30

the exhibitionist and his drag queen sister
are not quite as extroverted and hedonistic
as you may very well think deriving from
a spiritual abuse and deep-seated damage
done to the fragile identity during profound
significant periods of growth and development

31

"the coy" always appear to have some type
of sexual dysfunction or clinically-speaking
'fear of intimacy,' overcompensating by
role-playing (from a distance, which gives
them an advantage) speaking from both sides
of their mouth (mumbling...) or some other real
annoying sense of pseudo-modest 'intellectualization'

32

culture is the best we can expect out of human nature
as likewise civilization is the historical accumulation
of these selfsame customs, routines, rituals, and features

Hoard-a-culture

33

there's a perverse paradoxical psychological phenomenon
in the psychosocial environment where those who spread
the 'gossip and rumor' end up appearing in the herd-mentality
like 'the honest individual' while 'the victim' (the independent
thinker) simply minding his own business gets ostracized and alienated
that much further having absolutely no idea what he did to deserve this?

34

religion provides a certain sense of belief and belonging
but at the same time when wielded by the mediocre
masses a means for being mean and alienating and
passing instant judgment right when they leave
confession and head back to their delusions on their
exclusive dead end and meticulous obsessive lawns
in their one-upping homeowner's association where
they're humorless and take things way too serious
and don't 'absurdly' get they're the punchlines
to the mysterious riddle while their impossible
overbearing personalities make
them just like everybody else

35

the stuff that man brags of seems
like an exacerbation of his failures

The Rituals of Mummification

36

film-noir all those mistresses
and murdered husbands who
went missing cuz never had
the time for them and treated
them like possessions so time
for them to become possessed
and come out of hibernation
and reclaim their romantic
expressions and breathe again
and life and existence and property
while possession is three-fifths or
whatever the heck that expression?

37

they used to teach
with road hypnosis
to just dart your eyes
back and forth to keep
you up how drinking
coffee was a myth
and to crack open
your window a bit
to let in the cool
mountain air
when driving
a long haul

Hoard-a-culture

up & down
the coast
from los angeles to
seattle and the only
thing that mattered
was sleep when you'd
creep into one of those
bleak biscuit & gravy
truck stops with all
those nice & kind
cute pretty waitresses
and take a shower
and fall dead asleep
in your cabin with
your eye on your
gun or baseball bat
behind the curtain
across from that
mountain with
its top blown off
as turned out was
an active volcano
and now looks
something like
masada wondering
where the heck's
charlton heston?
steve mcqueen?
humphrey bogart?

The Rituals of Mummification

38

those old nostalgic black & white movie stars
had all these demons & skeletons in the closet
& taboo romantic extra-marital affairs & eventually
turned themselves into products which one could say
might be denial or just so damn tortured & tormented
didn't even care to look so far doing it all for the (p)art

39

a fine line between
porn & performing
& sincerely wanting
to just live (& to be
seen) happily ever after
the most brilliant ones
were the ones where
you couldn't tell
whether serious
or satire and in
the long-run
not really
sure if
any that
mattered

Hoard-a-culture

40

there is a baseline for movies in america
(if that's what you'd call them) of who has
better fireballs and explosions and computer
generated mythological characters and actresses
with the compulsion to expose their top and bottom
as their hourglass figures are ticking on the red carpet

41

felt so old (not for all the obvious reasons)
this morning suddenly doing the ymca dance
for your kid ahhh fuck it! and stick an esmerelda
marcos stamp on the envelope and send it out
to the irs; self-medication is just a big politically
correct word for wishing to just finally be content
in the moment flying the wind out in the kite as he
blows me away with all the facts and acts he has retained
about the revolutionary war one of the few that really
seemed to make any sense at all like that brilliant
absorbing performance everyone always seems
to forget with jack nicholson in *five easy pieces*

42

i sometimes love to watch some of those old
technicolor beach film surfer flicks where it
will show these rival teenager cliques really

The Rituals of Mummification

aggressively and combatively going at it
and trying to claim whose side of the beach
is whose and who owns it and which part
of the sea and wave is theirs and when
i deconstruct and breakdown and analyze
all of these and then apply how futile and silly
and similarly compare it to how almost every
great police-action or war began from a complete
disconnect and clueless lack of communication
one of man's weakest traits and characteristics
from ancient rome and egypt and the conquest
of the normans and ottomans and the middle
east and bold claim of how they were going
to drive the israeli's into the sea and world
war I and world war II and korea and all our
beliefs of how we were going to drive them
back to perceived parallels and vietnam and
infamous domino theory to stop the spreading
of communism even iraq and the conspiratorial
fictional weapons of mass-destruction and huge
surprise and shocker never were to be discovered
it's not too far of a stretch to make a direct comparison
to all these late 50's early 60's surfer fliks where perfectly
sculpted teenagers and their chicks were willing to go
all out and rumble and kill each other over territory and
wonder why they simply can't just be in the brilliant and
radiant sparkling iridescent beauty of the beach and sea?

43

think the instant panacea is to just simply look up desperately
right up at god but what if all that conflict of guilt and doubt
and poor self-image and hesitation kicks in and concerned
it might just be some dummy ventriloquist groucho with
mustache and cigar phil silvers in those big oversized
fogged-up camp director bifocals or just one of those
bizarre doris day and rock hudsons where they tried
to find the solution to all our spiritual and existential
problems in the safe and secure absurd plush technicolor
of suburbia, which in the long-run, will always inevitably
through repression and denial lead to a whole new other
set of psychological problems, like the climax of our baseline
all got so far and as high as this fantasy (of perceived happiness
and holiness) in postwar america right before the crises and tragedies
of the maddening, nihilistic, cultural, youth 'revolution,' while our
present day existence is simply pie-in-the-sky politicians projecting
(without even being aware of it, coincidentally and subconsciously)
pining to go back to the pinnacle of this post-war/pre-war patriotic
unrealistic, idealistic and literal and symbolic collective arrested
stage of development both setting up the stage for alternative
realities of functioning for those who will never ever fit in

The Rituals of Mummification

44

shattered seagulls soar over
the shoulders of the solitary
whitewashed buildings of
san francisco as you stare
out your window starving
secluded alone from your
beatdown room on eddy
in tenderloin and their
sailing figures and far
away calls feel like
playing hopscotch

in the eternal empty
blissful nothingness
of nowhere heaven

the bums at the library

janitor down the hall
mopping up the bathroom

the only soul you know
with a window to the city

slightly cracked
open just a little

to let in all buddhist suffering & sorrow
change of seasons and life-transitions

Hoard-a-culture

45

as it all comes
    around full-circle

with your kid
    the melting snow

bringing about
    a bizarre rebirth

a missing pair
    of binoculars

a can of silly string
    & one walkie-talkie

a little more sun
    & might find the other

46

today i tried to look up the first girl
i made-out with who was extremely
cute and pretty and seemed willing
supposedly we went to bed together
at a keg party in the 7th grade and her
girlfriends the next monday started calling
her a "slut" and she tried later on that day
desperately calling me up on the payphone
at the pizza place while hanging out with
my buddies because she wanted to prove

The Rituals of Mummification

to her mean girlfriends who in retrospect
in my opinion were the *real* sluts that we
were going out which we really weren't
and guess now i feel bad and guilty about
that but i suppose back then under all that
pressure not ready and a little scared and
totally overwhelmed with such responsibilities
and just wanted to still hang out with my buddies

the nice sicilian boys making the pizza
always making us feel welcome…

wondering why right now in my 40's i'm trying to look up
that really cute and pretty girl i made out with in the 7th grade

47

wanted to just hang out all day
at the pizza place in the clamor
and clang (like clockwork)
and self-soothing sound
of trains rushing in
at rush-hour from
grand central

48

the subtle slight leftover sound
of that babbling river tumbling
through rounds and rounds

Hoard-a-culture

of pop-up, chock-full
sprouting seasons

49

deep-down inside where somewhere
lies 'the mind…' likewise to never
underestimate the role that weather
played, the stirring (spirit and) soul
and necessary 'sense of' belonging

50

somehow within the moment
subconsciously knowing
how it can just take-off
without rhyme or reason
like a thief in the evening

51

the dusks
the stripmall
the synagogue
and pock-marked fog

The Rituals of Mummification

52

the silhouette
of whole cut-out village
and shortcuts at twilight

53

windswept birds on the wire
only happy when you're hollow

54

almost everything in childhood
which saved you was olfactory

in the medicine cabinet
the cupboard change of
seasons and ball field

those baseball cards
neatly wrapped with
that thin stick
of bubblegum

55

you kept neatly stored like objects
of desire in your pockets until you

Hoard-a-culture

flipped them all and got rid of them
the adrenaline flowing like crazy
bent over on your ripped skinned
knees in the sun-scorched school-
yard opposing rivals going at it
best friends rubbing each others
back for good luck with one
of the best players to hope
to make a major score

56

bazooka joe was a fugitive on-the-run

57

jesus christ when you think about it
was something of a 'self-fulfilling prophet'
so too were job and moses; poor righteous souls
naturally standing up for their rights and all that they know

58

the opposite of how they try to brainwash you

like in many ways how the punch line
always came way before the riddle

The Rituals of Mummification

59

to me flattery and praise always felt like an awfully strange
and aggressive way to manipulate but constructive criticism
coming from a friend or acquaintance always kind of felt like
i knew where they were coming from and how it was intended

60

certain expressions
sometimes they call them idioms
even when said in context end up
making you feel more separated
desperate alienated abandoned

such as "kismet" or "a penny for your thoughts"
as instantly feel the sensation of separation
anxiety disorder and wanting to 'turn off'
hostile, defensive, repulsed, and
needing to keep it all to myself

61

yet sometimes impossible after one of those
really cool and hip and avant-garde magazines
get back to me with their very formal and cookie-
cutter greeting of dear writer please don't submit
for at least 3 months and decide to very sarcastically
respond on the spot of which i got an auto response

and wrote something like dear auto response this is
an auto response to your auto response just wanted
to thank you a lot for getting back in touch and don't
be a stranger oi! 3-5 and for any true criminal or ex-con
who's been treated like a number or lost in the system
obviously means your bid and time gotta serve behind bars

the philosophers and psychologists and even school counselors
love to take the easy way out and refer to this as being something
of a "class clown" with such semantics as "acting-out" or "impulsive"
or "attention-seeking" or even "oppositional-defiant disorder" only
empirically don't know 'your side of the story' and who started it all
and can assure you never seen it or been there and are the exact ones
to know all mockery and sarcasm comes from a pretty damn sincere place…

62

these days in my dreams
simultaneously feel like
both friend and enemy

tell me something
i don't know
hail falls in the hall…

The Rituals of Mummification

63

one wonders if when
john glenn took off
to the moon left
a note in the milk
box for his kid
that said—"i'll
be back in
about a
week or
so, will
see you
then..."

ibid.
it should all be as placid as a puddle
as a kid scuttling through hysterical
taking off his mud boots and leaving
them in the foyer at dusk taking
long bubble baths in late-autumn
with his green pistol and tug boat

64

ibid.
snarling like sid vicious
waiting for the change
of seasons the ghosts
the madwomen no

Hoard-a-culture

rhyme or reason
swirling chimneys
and families returning
home roaming along
dusk highway from minor
league baseball in the bliss
of melancholy not really caring
who wins or loses or their destiny

ibid.
the most beautiful thing in america
was catherine ross; she only made
like 3 really good films like james
dean…the graduate, butch cassidy
& the sundance kid & the stepford
wifes, what was it with j. dean? rebel
without a cause, east of eden and giant
wonder if i had to do one of those really
futile and annoying match 'em up tests
like we used to have to do in elementary
and connect their similarities with a line
think i would put together the graduate
with rebel, butch cassidy with east
of eden and stepford wives with giant
kind of show their chronology and growth
and development; catherine ross and
jimmy dean should have been married

The Rituals of Mummification

65

dear samuel clemens:
where the fuck are the good triggers?

66

human nature (being a microcosm) precludes with its erratic behavior
and character there's absolutely no sense of fairness as what they deem
to be 'a democracy' or 'democratic government' is supposed to provide
a checks and balances, 'to serve and protect,' and semblance of sanity
and self-preservation but what if its machinations and how it functions
runs by just as corrupt dynamics and practice and nepotism and
deception and 'absurdly' what it all comes down to eventually
is who plays the role or plays the game just a little bit better

the wise man (through experience and wisdom or learned intuition)
is always wary of the consequences of a democracy and never
to become stuck or a slave or a statistic to the system

hitherto, think it's crazy when they try to sum
up different philosophers and their philosophies
(their belief system, moral and ethical thought
patterns, politics, schools, and methodologies)
as most likely just a mood he woke up
in (the damage human nature did to him
and just trying to get through this existence)

67

reverse descartes proof:
i know man is scum
'cuz whenever they
come to work for us
they steal our stuff
rings, faith, pain
killer, trust…

68

anti-proof #1

the very delicate and detailed sound of silverware
measures trauma and how reflective and lonesome

69

anti-proof #2

has anyone ever tried to drink
themselves under the table
below the image of
a noose and halo
under the moon?

The Rituals of Mummification

70

anti-proof #3

baby, i can't stop crying
and climbing the belltower
perfect day for fog and believe
delusions actually start from people's
desperate need to cling onto something…

who in fact really were the ringling brothers?

71

anti-proof #4

retorts–"you call me sweetie whenever you want to kill me!"

72

anti-proof #5

people always trying to come to terms
often forgetting the terms they're
trying to come to terms…
there's a fine line between two crooked points

73

alternative titles

1, on the self-image of wild animals
2. on the sex habits of border patrol
3, on sabbatical with the rabbinical rogue
4, on gardening hints of the tutor who still lives with his mother
5, on gossip & rumors worse than any religion
6, on the mating rituals of hollywood starlets & sex symbols
7, on the candidate who never existed
8, on how to squaredance or bunnyhop to the apocalypse
9, on how not to trust the flamboyant or eccentric
10, on feeling more connected with roadkill on the side of the road
11, on surviving and getting through this life
winding-up on the tightrope feeling more
safe & secure with fewer ways to cope
12, on taking a cruise to save the marriage
coming back like a funeral procession
with more questions than answers
13, on turning away from dysfunction
into the arms of strangers…

The Rituals of Mummification

74

girl from poland i really like a lot who we have a lot in common
like bushwick, brooklyn and philadelphia who i was talking to on
our cold windy lawn for a couple hours 'cause she is going to help
us with our gardening discovered a dead crow just lying there in the
middle of our hill and asked if she could have it. i said of course and
what are you going to do with it as long as you promise not to eat it.
she very casually said no and just liked the look of it and was probably
going to do something with the feathers and very delicately almost like
an egyptologist picked it up and placed it in a couple paper towels and
wrapped it up then took a couple more notes and took off. she also has
a tiller and now lives with her boyfriend and do hope he treats her well

she told me she used to work and farm up in buffalo
and thought whoah who the hell gardens and farms
in buffalo but what the hell do i know and told her
the only thing i know about buffalo is that great
indie film *buffalo 66* about that ex-convict who
returns home and turns out in the long-run really
does have a heart of gold and it's just the fucked-
up dysfunctional family he is forced to have to
contend with and brings out the worst in him
and causes him to act-out and do some
crazy shit which i really was able to relate
to and another brilliant indie called *stranger
than paradise* about this polish girl who comes
from poland to the lower east side to live with her
city slickster cousin and then eventually moves
in during the winter months with her aunt on lake

Hoard-a-culture

eerie out in cleveland and said she would definitely
check them out and her boyfriend would just break
into the computer or do some criminal shit
to get them and felt pretty good about that

a little later on she asked me if we wanted
to plant parsley and i told her no and always
just seemed like the leftover crumbs on the plate
after you eat a cheeseburger and could tell
by her non-verbals was not too thrilled with
my answer and told her i guess it's good if
you like mix it into some potato salad but
probably for now will hold off on the parsley
and deflected with our mutual love for cilantro
and can put it in practically anything like tuna
fish something that my old half-crazed rich girl
friend from the upper east side who claimed she
was a zionist made for me and just based on
those midnight sandwiches thought i loved her

we spoke about the importance of parogies
and kielbasa and sour cream and things
which really actually taste like things
and gave her my connections to all
the secret haunts and polish enclaves
in greenpoint, brooklyn and the lower
east side and made me want to just
jump right in my car and zoom for
a couple mindless hours straight
to that diner for a combination platter
and just sit in there blissfully anonymous

The Rituals of Mummification

for hours in the window like i used to and
lose myself and gaze at all the madmen
and hustlers i knew and put the whole
damn half-crazed universe in perspective

then she started to make me feel a little low
or down-in-the-dumps and doubt her as asked
if she might be able to bring over her boss and
talked about his reputation and had all this experience
and was something of a legend and told her i never really
felt too comfortable around the legends and preferred the
presence of bums and from my experience for some strange
and fucked-up reason find they present with the exact same
hackneyed patterns; how they always instantly check you
out and act all paranoid and suspicious (usually from their
shortcoming weaknesses and ignorance and distorted even
delusional thought patterns) and all hostile and have pre-
conceived notions and pass instant judgment and conclusions
and criminalize you even when they don't know a thing about
you or more so themselves and ironically right when you're
on your own property and said think i'll have to pass
on the offer as believe it's really just a one man job

at the end of our discussion she suddenly
asked me 'what do i really know about farming'
which didn't quite understand the line of questioning
and said i really try not to get too complicated like
ph levels and so on but me and my son are really
good at watering and maintaining and just simply
want to see the corn and pumpkins grow and there
was a certain amount of silence and awkwardness

Hoard-a-culture

but i don't know guess i might have felt a little
resentful by this very formal question and she
seemed just as introverted and pleased with it

when she left i ended up having mixed feelings
and if anything felt good to bullshit and reflect
and get stuff off my chest with a therapist
you're not exactly sure if you trust or not
and tried to imagine those pumpkins and
corn coming up but just couldn't and hope
with the whimsical and erratic nature of man
and their behavioral patterns of what they always
pretend to offer she in fact actually even shows up

75

this morning i was feeling all down-in-the-dumps i guess
'cuz just the common theme of schmucks who never ever
get back to me or make promises they never keep and
putting you in that unenviable "hamlet dilemma" and
wonder why eric b. erickson the infamous psychologist
(no not the president for *hairclub for men*) never spoke
about this in his convenient stages of 'human growth
and development' then all of a sudden came on from
a leftover muted infomercial from the night before
the very happy and holy christie brinkley and
chuck norris almost like one of those pods that
come tumbling out of one of those bubblegum
machines in childhood and not coincidently
had on one of those plastic smiles from ear

The Rituals of Mummification

to ear even after she had been divorced from
'the piano man,' and his series *walker texas
ranger* had been taken off the air and swear
it was all like some sort of half-crazed out-
of-control fucken control-freak cult and must
have showed "practically" every half-crazed pasty
upstanding citizen in america on all-fours manically
working every freaken part of the body (the gluteus
maximus, maximum gluteus, glutes, gizzards, pupicks,
and buttocks) and were out-of-control…divorcees, old
gigolos, past borderline girlfriends and joey butuaffuco
and when these true-blue loco fanatics were done they
showed them of course that much more confident and
sure of themselves and start wondering why i liked them
so much more when they were down on their luck and not
so sure of themselves then brought in the sample scenarios
of course of them all jogging happily ever after with those
elastic smiles through the perfectly manic/cured park strolling
romantically hand in hand along shore and not sure why for
some strange reason had walker the texas ranger suddenly
feeding cattle and kicking some rubber dummy which he
just happened to have hanging in his undecorated living
room with no pictures on the wall then i swear maybe got
it backwards or wrong very conveniently all money-back
guarantee risk-free in one fell swoop like some new dance
craze sweeping the nation folding up their beds and neatly
pushing them under this beating healing multi-aerobic
machine made to work and tone every part of
the body most especially the heart and soul

Hoard-a-culture

76

people are so phony at funerals and are just faking
they know nothing about mourning and just trying
to keep up appearances; matter of fact ironically
don't have a sincere bone in the body and like
to just bury them and start my own private
resurrection (some of them with their
fragmented and brainwashed thought
pattern even parasitic and vindictive
which they believe to be their own
spiritual closure) then take off early
to pick up my own personal platter
at the diner which will include something
like a reuben and fries and seltzer maybe
take a shower like christopher walken just
come out of prison and lay in my own safe
and secure sarcophagus naked and beaten
within my pristine immaculate bedroom
with the window slightly opened and tv
turned to spring training the only thing
which really holds any true meaning
to the life cycle and being and eternity
instead of frankincense and myrrh
thousand island dressing and
a leftover squeezed lemon

the natives down in sarasota…

The Rituals of Mummification

77

i just love that image
of all those old timers
just sitting at the wishing
well in the middle of the mall
with all those glistening coins
tossed in the fountain by romantics
and delinquents sincerely wishing
and praying for a better existence
and they got that look on their face
with eyes glazed over like please
just leave me the fuck alone and
seen it all and just grateful that
their wives are all giving them
a couple moments in shopping
and no crises or psychodrama
surrounded by all those very
single-minded and serious
mall walkers, sluts in short
shorts and maintenance with
their water bottles spraying
the artificial made-to-look
natural flora and whether
someone picks them
up or not all good
might provide a
little downtime
little breathing time
and like that feeling

Hoard-a-culture

of feeling stranded
and no one to be
responsible for
and irrelevant
and doesn't matter
and all the better
a certain kind
of postmodern
wasted and wired
version of buddha

78

after the constant madness of such domestic
shit like asshole neighbors having absolutely
nothing to do with and no traits or characteristics
or resemblance with those parables from the bible
or once again our accountant fucking up our taxes
when ironically we are so damn responsible you take
great pleasure in simply just watching some gorgeous
and graceful high school girl jogging past your window
with her freewheeling flowing hips and swinging elbows
and ponytail bobbing back and forth some time around
5:31 first day of spring catching cuba vs. tampa bay
making me spring straight out of my easy chair
and race down the hall and watch her disappear
to the horizon. she knows exactly what she's
doing to the whole male population and makes
life worth living as there's something really to be

The Rituals of Mummification

said about some girl with the perfect figure and her
ponytail bobbing back and forth taking off to the horizon

79

what next? we now find out
quaker oats with that portrait
of that very honest puritan quaker
is getting sued based on the fact
that they misled the public over
a very specific ingredient? makes
me wanna just deflate a football
and win the superbowl! comes
down to the only one i can
trust are jimmy cagney
and humphrey bogart
who used to get into
big drunken brawls
the night before
they made some
of their biggest
blockbuster films
what's that again?
public enemy?
i'm a yankee
doodle dandy?
casablanca
and the
maltese

Hoard-a-culture

falcon?
best friends
even brothers
will betray you
& now not even
a bullet can
stop you
film noir
was the heart
& soul of it all
those great intellectual
lonesome madmen
barely hanging on
due to trauma & loss
forced to live
in the shadows
unfairly, unjustly
ignored and accused
of the wrong identity
always forgot his name
i'm sure for some pure
subconscious reason
third man, stranger
adolph menjoue &
edward g. robinson

The Rituals of Mummification

80

all the great mathematicians
& philosophers & scholars
the ol' time classic comedians
imprisoned till the end of time
pressure-washing babylon

81

so hard to explain irony and satire
to the mundane masses and those
who just simply will never get it

82

most conclusions are based on false impressions…

83

how to become royalty
a madman, president

84

how all great inventions really came
from the sublimation of a very specific
spiritual and psychological oppression

Hoard-a-culture

85

how yiddish expressions pretty much say
and encompass it all; not just the necessary
and needy definition but also within the moment
the mood and musicality and meaning and sense
of humor, which adds so much more nuance and
dimension, better yet, subtle good-natured sarcasm
which really is the best and most complete type of in-depth
description that helps to fully explain 'manic' high-expressed emotion

86

drinking seltzer in the static
        some-
     where
  between bedford
stuyvescent,
brooklyn
  & krakow,
poland
    when the letters
        stopped
            coming...

The Rituals of Mummification

87

with all that fear
& loss of freedom
what other choice
did you have but
to become famous?

88

a perverted usher
at the 57th st. art's movie
theater in upper-manhattan

89

how to fall back in love
with your wife and not
take her for granted

90

how to not get hung-up
in all the guilt & bullshit
& brainwash passed-down
from generation to generation

Hoard-a-culture

91

draw the curtain
& you're right in
her dressing room

92

film-noir is the figure behind the smoke & mirrors & shadow & fog
it's the primitive & erratic dichotomy & contradiction between fragile
character & behavior & the aggressive self-interest of human nature
the psyche uncovered & the raw & naked nightmare in the motel
in the mansion of the madman of the millionaire the night dresser
with the gun & bible & shot of bourbon & blowing out the candle

when the subconscious gets exposed some-
where between role play & the real world

93

all those impossible seductive girls
from childhood turning into these very
respectful and responsible ('virtuous')
mother figures (how you figure?)

still not so convincing
still just out of reach

The Rituals of Mummification

94

a mathematical equation where the means
never justify the end because in truth and
reality there is no beginning and no end

95

they are nice and kind and generous
(and turn themselves into martyrs)
at their own convenience…

but consider 'the law of opposites'
inputting contrary negative
factors into the equation

and not by coincidence how quickly
flattery becomes criticism coming from
the same insecure character and behavior

96

if look deep enough in existence your dreams
turn to nightmares and nightmares to dreams…

Hoard-a-culture

97

what is reality?
reality! reality! reality! reality!
and the more you repeat it no reality

98

just barely hanging in there and never giving up
to a certain extent is the definition of 'perseverance'
and 'courageous' with no one to fall back on or support
us and looking back at this very challenging phase of existence
never forgetting will decide in the present whether to be or not to be…

99

a ghost forgetting to remember
(trying to remember to forget)
the things which matter most

100

how to make…
fresh-roasted vegetables
straight from your garden

The Rituals of Mummification

101

self-low
thing's
a mother

how to get-on…

Home Economics

passing through the netherworld

"There's ways of killing yourself without killing yourself"

—Saturday Night Fever

The Rituals of Mummification

*

On the making of fable or home movies:

7 older aristocratic women in sequins
dexterously bend over to peek feverishly
through the keyhole to watch some younger
man who's actually a third cousin they used
to baby sit for in the suburbs undress until
perfectly naked. they think back to days
of innocence but also a strange curiosity
still bent over dreaming and fantasizing
in their old-fashioned decadent hallway

*

he suddenly breaks out in sweet song
as their fingers all secretly naturally
make their way down to their sweet
spot that sticky snatch to the holiest
of holes and then each one of them
throw themselves on the fire like
perfectly cut sappy logs one by one
by one by one until it all transforms
into the most delicate and delicious
perfumed aroma, crawling up the
chimney and sprinkling over the mad
silhouetted rainy dark town at dusk

*

all those wraparound porches, trap doors, and
rear set of creaking stairs; the ghostly vestibules

Home Economics

and secret chambers hidden up there, secluded
with just one tiny porthole set back in the slanted
roof; ghost stories and tales of antiquity and abuse

*

country wraparound porches ran around
from the dew of morning to the dew of dusk
undulating lawn which runs down to the lake
to the swamp and lagoon we paddled through

*

through whispering stillness
of existence and evolution
prayer and promises to
make sure it all be true

*

the hush of lily pads
and swoop of egrets
penetrating skeleton
change of seasons

*

straddling the wings of a dragonfly through the blues

*

the ping-pong of bullfrogs
right before the curtain
of night draws down

The Rituals of Mummification

*

flashing neon of fireflies
with internal organs
stripped-down...

*

the train comes shuffling through
with an offer too good to be true

like model glue pharmacies on the corner
who used to sell ice cream sodas and heroin

*

the girl who has been hurt and betrayed way too many times
before; whose heart has been broken way too many times
before turns to breaking up stable and affluent marriages
while they all earn a reputation and all turn to a gossip
and rumor (not just them but the ones spreading it)
and last heard moved to the well-kept good looking
motels by the babbling brook on the edge of town

*

by the comic shops and cathedrals

by the thick bank of fog
on the tombstones
on the cornfield

in the valley
of the gorge
on the river

Home Economics

*

the institutions along with all the factories and mansions
have all shut down; the schools and the slaughterhouses

*

the paper mills
and silver mines

*

the mannequins only come out at night
in the halo of lamplight in what they like
to refer to as a city but really just the pity
of all that remains after industry leaves
cross-seas like a thief in the evening

and make names for themselves like
forgotten fiancees, brides left at the alter
and hookers; what other choice do they have as
everything's on layaway and all's poverty-stricken

*

gravediggers enter the gates of chinese buffet
with that tired and drained look on their face
check their shovels in with the hatcheck girl
and dead to the world make their way
to their tables still with all the mud
and soil and newly-buried spirits
of the universe on their clothes
will order a highball; why
the hell not? union job

The Rituals of Mummification

*

survival becomes something of a cross
between old hobby shops and the state
courthouse which used to be a quaint
old town and out-of-town convicts
who have chosen to settle down

*

faceless older woman who's one of those office clerks
(secretary, accountant, medical records...) and apparently
having not a whole heck of a lot to live for anymore heard
hollering at the top of her lungs, still not been confirmed
if a suicide or not with arms and limbs flailing in the river
which has flooded over and rambles past the police barracks
and tasty cream while happens so suddenly and quickly still
not sure if a fantasy or reality, a ghost or human being, as all

a part of the same scene and some young muscular heroic courageous
kid, doesn't even think about it, naturally and instinctively leaps in to
save her and last heard ironically developed pneumonia at the hospital

*

old pedophiles spend the rest of their days in the basement
looking at tarnished clippings and articles trying to piece
together and figure out where it all went wrong

they used to be in one of the wars

Home Economics

*

gorgeous blonde-haired salt-of-the-earth girls
literally trample down the hill behind
the auto body shop to pay their rent

they are to die for and are as much
a part of the environment as the
stray roosters and chickens

*

the priest seems no different than the drug dealers
than the madmen and molesters and jury and judge
and if you choose to judge them, would simply be
playing yourself out as all got tricks up their sleeves
and coping and surviving like some lost little half-
crazed dysfunctional town where everyone knows
everyone else, thus choosing to keep things under-
cover for purposes of functioning and self-preservation

they've seen better days and been dead for ages
and know the hustle and everything in between

*

they spend evenings on front porches dazed-out
on painkiller beneath pagoda bug zappers sizzling
and electrocuting and zapping the creatures of
the night completely turned-off and oblivious

the lady of the house smokes cigars

The Rituals of Mummification

*

sew i guess you got martha washington
the mother of the united states of america
or was that mamie eisenhower or marilyn
monroe or bessie smith or bessie bluestein
making her m & m cookies in jamaica queens
or maybe that's just simply me mutely wailing
while diligently knitting the addendum to the
declaration of independence or codependence
of dope dependence or obituaries to the horrors
of our present day opiate addiction while the rest
of the porch full of drunks and grifters and runaways
and fugitives on-the-run and stray dogs passed-out
from the sun across from the broken down casinos
and homeless hoteliers with drinking problems
and those unruly brothers with hearts of gold
out chasing tornadoes and finally just can't
fight it no more and nodding-out in the model
glue fumes from a battalion of fighter ships and
jet planes with proud insane generals made up
of jigsaw puzzles in picture frames and pieces
missing where their hearts and souls should be
making fun of mumbling scholars who can't speak
up for themselves looking to be saved and redeemed

and the delinquents & fire setters
taking the day off due to the heat

Home Economics

*

stray dogs as well-known and as much
a part of the scene as anybody else

*

old timers and their widows from the old country
come out every weekend morning marching
to the beat of their own drummer

to some ancient festival and solstice
under the influence and disoriented

*

their grandchildren; the studs and gigolos and delinquents
from the neighborhood make fun of them and mournfully
modestly mock–"they're walking…" which really means
they're marching in another one of these damn things like
wind-up zombies and there's nothing they can do about it

*

the stately victorians have all turned to law offices
for townies with chemical-dependency problems
and rich boys who can't keep themselves out of
trouble constantly being brought up on gun charges
hard time remembering the past especially nostalgia

The Rituals of Mummification

*

spoiled persian son whose parents own the all-night boxcar
diner beneath the mountain seduces all the college boys
coming in on dusty buses from the big city; they know
all his secrets and what he does for a living, rigid and
repulsed by his need to flaunt his contemporary moires
and ways of being; his active-rebellion to custom and
tradition even in a bit of denial and can't stand it; they
blame everyone like some strange guilt by association

*

the game warden comes in who used to be
a gym teacher and work part time for the state
police inappropriately humping the wheel to his pickup

he and his wife who is an angel
gave birth to sons constantly
on-the-run from the law

*

there's news they're closing down
the dump and putting up a nuclear plant

*

real-life phantoms come out somewhere between
the forest and the flickering light of the old shadowy
movie theater bringing light to the holy haunted dawn

Home Economics

*

all you hear is the sweet somber melancholy muffled
blast of foghorns and trainhorns with a lingering sort of lost
trailing echo trembling and trickling through the town that hugs
your naked lonesome bones and makes you feel right at home

little less lost and hollow and for the moment
gives the illusion you might actually belong

*

when you get home you will pin yourself up
like one of those old rusty badminton racquets
last of the maddening flapping butterflies
of the season jesus on the cross brooding
daydreaming about that stream which used
to run behind the library and merchant shops
and whenever the rain came down would fill
it all up giving it all its character and folklore
and personality whose sudden out-of-control
raging currents of insanity allowed you to finally
have feelings of belief and liberation and freedom

have bedbugs ever said
before they went to bed–
"don't let the madmen bite!"

*

soon the pretty waitresses and bank tellers
who break hearts who guys throw
it all away for will wake up...

The Rituals of Mummification

A Hx Of Stream Of Consciousness

like jack kerouac's lost choruses

"The sun will shine in my backdoor some day..."

—Grateful Dead

The Rituals of Mummification

#1

Where do butterflies go at night?
they say that jesus died for us
well if that be so how come
no one showed up to try
and help him off
the whole fucked
up self-interested
& self-absorbed
thing about
humanity
& adds so
much more
to the tragic
spiritual loss
marilyn monroe
man in the mirror
& prince all died
from an overdose
all by their lone
some say a quarter
of his heart is buried
in sacre-coeur up on
top of monmartre
while 'so much
depends' & grows
in the mist & fog
of the cobblestone
through the key

A Hx Of Stream Of Consciousness

hole of the holy
haunted forest
wonder why
montana,
dodge,
cheyenne,
or sioux falls
never got a
professional
ball club?
say that
babe ruth
spent the
rest of his
life just
waiting
for a
phone
call
that in
the long
run just
would
never
come

The Rituals of Mummification

#2

America ain't got
actresses or actors
anymore! they all
just do porn with
their downtime
on smartphones
nearly 1,000,000
people lost their
lives in the civil war
black men will start
losing theirs from
excessible force
of police forces
'cuz it's
summer
just above
& right below
the mason-dixon
teddy roosevelt the
rough rider was 46
when he took office
(our economy is run by
the strip mall & single
mom strippers strung
out on methadone
with suffering sons
now mandated to see
school social workers)

A Hx Of Stream Of Consciousness

standard & poors just
plummeted about 600
due to great britain
leaving the union
(still though
sure can get
scrumptious
chocolate chip
& orange scones
& clotted cream
& *english twinings*)
our republican
candidate for
commander
in chief
a man
of the people
who will bring
jobs back to america
goes over there
to christen his
most recent
golf resort
& after
bragging
about how
much he is
worth gives
them mock
support ironically

The Rituals of Mummification

looking exactly like
the joker from batman
with his madman smirk
& big wig & reality show
orange face makeup
do you think if a
survey was done
anyone would know
cathryn hepburn
& jason robards
were in the film
version of 'long
days journey?'
who walter
pigeon
victor
mature
were?

#3

O drawbridge please let in
the rest of the blessed fog
horns that suddenly start
blooming out of nowhere
in the deep dense wee hours
of the morning and yes guess
i'm one of them who agree sir
lawrence olivier was one of

A Hx Of Stream Of Consciousness

the greatest actors of all
time even way before he
got his title of knight &
richard burton turned
to wine & developed
his drinking problem
& histrionics so hallelujah
why not let the minors
do underage drinking
as they simply add so
much more to the ambiance
& romance & madness
of the tavern & take off
dungarees & leather
in active-rebellion
to assert & establish
identities as all just
go around once maybe
a couple more times if get
lucky while it all just tastes
so much better in the form of
leftovers coming out the refrigerator
at 3 in the morning when standing
there naked solitary & frost forming
on the chilly comfy crystal lattice
with blasts & last blast haloes
of heat from rambunctious
radiators gathering behind
the tinctured colored glass
bottle collection sitting flush

The Rituals of Mummification

against the secret solitary
twinkling street lamp
of the winter season
of sleepy hollow
& the whole
holy town
dressed up
& down in
delicate shadow
smells like sweet
chimney smoke
when for the first
time forever you
feel contented
in the moment
with really having
nowhere else to go
when the only thing
to fear or really love
at all is the open
& exposed
heart & soul
still not knowing
for sure which one
is abbot & which
one is costello
as if any that
ever mattered
jimmy stewart
suicidal fragile

A Hx Of Stream Of Consciousness

taking a flying
leap at midnight
into that foghorn
river when he felt
like he had nothing
left to live for no joke
mr. jones mr. coffee
mr. janny weizmuller

#4

3 officers killed, 3 officers injured, 1 suspect down
in baton rouge, louisiana; seems to be an everyday
happenstance in america & you just go numb
more so concerned about no one showing up
anymore to the mom & pop hamburger stand
which triggers ones mortality & melancholia
& what happens after they just decide it's
not worth it anymore to close their doors?

#5

The once adventurous & dangerous
borough of brooklyn has now become
a very wealthy & gentrified suburb
& to be able to afford a brownstone
gotta be bougeous soulless schmuck
alienating asshole multi-millionaire
whose dad passed down his plastic

The Rituals of Mummification

pick-up stick business as this
is what it means as well to be
an exclusive member of the coop
as just seem to kind of have that
all mixed-up & backwards?

#6

Looking back in retrospect at all of those
brilliant ol' time slapstick comedians such
as d.w. griffith, w.c. fields, charlie chaplin,
buster keaton, find them to be some of
the most valuable mvp american icons
of all time just as much as any president
like washington & lincoln & theodore
& fdr & to hold & carry just as much
sentiment & sincerity & nostalgia
as anybody else & guess it's true
there's a fine line between tragedy
& comedy while humor heals all

#7

Punchlines seemed
           to collectively
placate & calm us down
as much as any new deal

A Hx Of Stream Of Consciousness

#8

A note stuck to our refrigerator
for the summer–"swim lessons
and learn to tie shoelaces" lying
back on our gushy couches with
the lightning flashing & thunder
during the evening catching tv
with my kid & a failed military
coup in turkey decide to explain
the whole contemporary hx of
the middle east which includes
as well the country of y'israel
made it our homeland after the
holocaust & how arabs claimed
they were gonna drive the jews
into the sea & using their wits
& strategy & comradery took
down 5-6 arab countries in 6
blessed days based on the fact
that they couldn't get along &
always fighting each other &
literally wiped out their whole
air force before they could
even get off the ground &
in the air & he seemed so
proud & beaming & asked
is that what we're about
& naturally responded
pretty much so…

The Rituals of Mummification

#9

Turns out 15 years later
looking back at marriage
my wife actually resembles
that really pretty cute jewish
girl with the long hair and great
smile i just picked up at the social
at the roller disco in summer camp
and romantically grabbing her hand
skating round and round and round
and round hits of plumes of perfume
and shampoo sweeping up the senses

she was from my hometown
and the dreams i imagined…

#10

Knew she was the right girl
for me cuz a really bad border
line girl i just got off of told her
she used to call me rough
around the edges while
she instantly blurted–

"i think *she's* rough
around the edges!"

A Hx Of Stream Of Consciousness

#11

Wife's mother who got abandoned
by her husband who was a banker
and a casanova and ended up
marrying the last woman he
cheated with and turning from
a reformed jew to conservative
living in a huge apartment
of hoarding in the bronx
and whenever she had
to serve her breakfast or
supper would give it to her
and repeat that commercial
like some sort of pithy psalm–
"you want it, you got it, toyota!"
then like everything else in miserable
life and existence, it just got boiled
down to 'toyota' like some hallelujah
from the congregation or amen from
the synagogue left them all by their
lonesome and the only thing worth
living for was that 12th floor terrace
in the bronx overlooking the park...

The Rituals of Mummification

#12

She still looks just as pure and pretty
when she comes out of her flowery
shower when i asked her to marry
me taking her to perkofiev's *romeo
& juliet* at radio city on valentine's
and maybe a bit buzzed under the influence
of some cocktail at intermission suddenly
popped the infamous question in the middle of
the performance and pulled me out to the lobby
to make sure she had heard me right wasn't sure
if i heard myself right and right on the spot looked
into my eyes and said yes and we just took off
walking hand in hand down all those vacant
shadowy streets from lincoln center to grand
central vanderbilt avenue which sounds so
significant but really the filthy sooty pot
of gold at the end of the rainbow where
bums & billionaires go and the shortest
and smallest avenue no one seems to ever
really know or maybe just the destination
of those processions of maddening taxis
madmen always in transition or in a state
of constant flux from the insane metropolis
to the fictional and ridiculous suburbs and
practically had nothing to say to each other
as if silent and in shock haunted hollow
strolling somewhere towards our future

A Hx Of Stream Of Consciousness

#13

You wake up in the morning with a throbbing
pain in your neck but are placated and well-
up to baroque while listening to the forecast
from montpelier to montreal (in everything
we been through and had to get through
in just this way we made it) and imagine
jesus crucified on a razor by gillette
wrangler tells us to just be comfortable
to just be yourself (whoever the hell that is)
and these idiots all dressed up in their knight
and king and wench costumes for the renaissance
fare come on over your television; you are calmed
by the morning sun just burning off the fog watching
the path the fragile mist takes slipping down the mountain

#14

And so it gets to a certain
point in your life where
it even hurts at the top
of your arthritic psycho
somatic spine to laugh
and cry and live and
die to fart and squeeze
out a sweet song of sighs
in midlife at midnight
in all your arrested stages

The Rituals of Mummification

of development dreaming
of dreaming of dreaming
of dreaming of being
coiled in the fetal position
as a toddler in your sky-blue
cowboy & indian pajamas
with those boots on the
bottom after a feast of
pork chops and baked
apples and onions— what
were they called again ma?

#15

Dear Erica,

Seeing the purple
perennials in the back
yard through the blinds
of our bedroom window
reminds me of your
purple sundress you
put on every summer

#16

You get a letter—

"Fox on the loose
in East Montpelier.

A Hx Of Stream Of Consciousness

I bumped into Anna and Rose.
They're working w/ students
    Can't get casper off the slide…"

#17

Wanna write this children's story
where some heroic paul bunyon
like character just simply
stands at home plate
in the middle of the
misty night and
whacks it out of
the ballpark "you can
kiss that baby good
bye" and it just sails
right over the smoggy
lights up onto the moon
which sits cradled up
there all by its lone
some and the rest
of the story trying
to find and locate
it most likely having
made it up there some
where around the stars
the rest of the story
just showing that
sliver of moon

The Rituals of Mummification

hanging up there
and knowing there's
a lovely little leather
rawling's baseball
rolling back & forth

#18

I remember
being back
in grade
school
in the
1970's
& them
actually
asking
& surveying
us what we
thought should
be the national
animal of america
as it was a run
off between
like the horse
& bald eagle
& we know who
eventually won
in the long-run

A Hx Of Stream Of Consciousness

& remember
taking rainy
day thundering
buses on field
trips from new
york to philadelphia
to see the cracked liberty
bell & u.s. mint & black
girls getting stuck clucking
in the bus bathroom returning
home with a couple glistening
sterling silver susan b anthony's
not knowing exactly who she was
but feeling solid stuffed deep down
in my dungaree pocket maybe like
golda meir that pretty handsome
prime minister from israel when
things seemed to really matter

#19

Wow america
assassinated
and stole
practically
everything
from me
hearing it
in disbelief

The Rituals of Mummification

sputtering
over my rock
& roll station
in high school
filling up gas
for my station
wagon at sun
down on the strip
mall somewhere
between the toy
store and tavern
where i grew up
and kept it all in
and wonder if this
is where my arrested
stage of development began
those miniature light bulbs
scattered all over and hidden
deep within the high shag
carpet of bedroom closets
them all suddenly disappearing
and missing-in-action either be
coming doctors or drug addicts
the latter ironically always
seeming so much smarter
and more compassionate

A Hx Of Stream Of Consciousness

#20

She was the first girl
i played hangman with
the first girl i hung out with
the first girl i walked home with
the first girl who kept an extra
bottle of hot sauce in her pocket
book in case we needed it and
from what i heard recently
she became one of these
really brilliant cut-throat
attorneys and the way
i been feeling think
be the perfect client
hope she'd represent
or even for that matter
remember me as was
always one of those
kids in school they
told their mothers
was a real nice guy
and even went out
of their way to bake
a slice of baklava...

The Rituals of Mummification

#21

Back then felt like neil young would save
our soul and in many ways he did—
now i just dream of a home-cooked meal

all those records
flipped through
at the mall

returning home with
quadrophenia
on the bus

we ironically
hysterically
stole

a whole wardrobe full of
polo shirts your mother
didn't recall

maroon corduroy pocket
full of razorblades
and candles

made something
of yourself
in detention hall

free/dumb...
never a last time to make a first impression
being a wise ass meant everything...

A Hx Of Stream Of Consciousness

equate empty pool on pitt st.
to an autumn evening
vacant lonely solitary happy

(like a candle flickering
in the russet windows
of those gold brick

buildings
in the bronx
right around the reservoir)

what does it really mean
to get out on good behavior?
to find your savior to save her

#22

Ripping shirts off saints
who started the fight
at the chinese buffet?
"i've been rich and
i've been poor..."
who said that?
was it billie holiday
or ella fitzgerald
all just trying
to get back
to that brilliant
buzzed moment
shortest distance

The Rituals of Mummification

between two points
ain't necessarily
always a straight
line but crooked
& reflective
& romantic
& high

#23

Nothing seems
    to really matter these days
when you turn on your tv
& got cocktease couples getting
boxes delivered of pre-cooked
gourmet food & flashcards
on how to prepare it, mean
wasn't the whole point
to be spontaneous?
inspired & motivated
& make something
from the heart
& romantic
they got a
special club
where they
pick out
the wine
for you

A Hx Of Stream Of Consciousness

bottle
by bottle
based on
your very
selective
interests
yiick! so
a delight
in every
swig?
i suppose
guaranteeing
you a safe
& secure
existence
buzz, blood
good drunk
& less of a
hangover?
what next
for marriage
proposals give
it to you in the
form of a fortune
cookie no matter
how the cookie
crumbles?

The Rituals of Mummification

#24

In politics
it really
is all
a
bout
per
cep
tion
&
who
's
less
likely
(or more
potential)
towards
deception

#25

In brookland
ebullient tom
boys with angel
lick mischievous
laughter control
the neighbor/hood
& head back home

A Hx Of Stream Of Consciousness

ward to brown
stones at dusk
past the virgin
marys locked
up in chicken
wire so the de'link
wents won't get to it

#26

Where does the circus lady
with the beard, that man who
runs the strongest man in the
world with great big sledge
hammer and bell, the acrobat,
tightrope worker go at the end
of the day? know they can't get
a mortgage like a hard-working
industrious captain in the mafia
but forced to settle for a bed in
the boiler room of his sister's
basement in brighton beach
brooklyn feeling constant guilt
and conflict for being an imposition
but what'ya gonna do? doing his best

The Rituals of Mummification

#27

The sun goes
down over
vestibules
& those
silhouettes
of cathedrals
& derricks
on the river
(made us
feel right
at home
with a sense
of belonging)
was our own
silent solemn
version of
confession

#28

Everyone had their
secret connection
& something they
were deeply ashamed
of like hearing those
sudden anguished
hollow howls

A Hx Of Stream Of Consciousness

coming from
somewhere
down the hall
like throwing rocks
backwards cuz was
so damned lonely
out of windows
already shattered

#29

The godfather
played by brando
in "the godfather"
never quite
made it out
of the forest
and bit
the dust
with his
grand
son
both in
hysterics
living
happily
ever
after
when

The Rituals of Mummification

jimmy
stewart
desperately
clutched
& held
onto his
cherubic
daughter
for dear
life in a
wonder
full life
grateful
& teary-
eyed
a true-blue
blessing in
disguise
& had
everything
to do with
mortality
might
even
take
a blind
audrey
hepburn
(real-life
blind

A Hx Of Stream Of Consciousness

leading
the blind)
to keep
me from
feeling
so damn
lonely!

#30

So what if in fact
all life is a great big act
a delicate dance where
you ask for her hand
and still not sure if
ever got a response
on a spiritual and existential level?
(they're all just a bunch of devils!)
some futile, frustrating puzzle which
lies somewhere between faith & fate
and all it all comes down to upon
reflection are a series of pillow
talk sessions with girls you
were convinced at least
at that exact time
and moment you
sincerely loved

The Rituals of Mummification

#31

How would you define a badboy?
a deep-down passionate romantic
at heart? oppositional-defiant?
anti-authority? wouldn't
even know what those
terms mean as just
busy surviving
who would be
considered in the
category of badboy?
jimmy dean in "rebel without
a cause?" brando in 'streetcar?'
even jon voight in "midnight
cowboy" always just be
yond their control just
trying to make it
& make names
for themselves

#32

They say that over the hill
fake aristocrat he tried
to pick up outside her
steaming sweltering
manhattan condo
with that brilliant

A Hx Of Stream Of Consciousness

surreal maddening
power-struggle
& sleazy rendez-
vous of denial
which lasted just
under 3 minutes
landed her in 1969
best supporting actress

#33

Have had so many relationships like that
(which felt just as substantial for all those
exact reasons i wasn't supposed to have)

#34

Women are the concrete solution
to the abstract problem of living
the whimsical punchline to the
unsolved complicated riddle
providing instant proof
& detail & meaning to
all the routines & rituals
of the brutal triviality of
everyday being & reality
the risks man is willing

The Rituals of Mummification

to take for a little escape
& possible chance for
laughs & romance…

#35

The great thing about sex
is that it accepts 'practically'
everything life rejects looking
out like some edward hopper
from your pink kitchen naked
bone-tired to the subway cars

erotic relationships always
brought you so much closer
to the culture of civilization

#36

Getting back
to brando
not as fond
of "the wild ones"
cuz just seemed
more of a thug
and a little less
sympathetic
than perhaps
when he grew

A Hx Of Stream Of Consciousness

up hollering once
more out-of-control
under the el in 'last tango'

#37

The traveling carnival makes its way into town
having forgotten its freaks and animals
just empty rattling flatbeds which
somehow makes you feel
alive once more...

#38

Looking for a second job in "manufacturing" swear i saw one
for *genie bottle repair* and knew i could do that at the drop
of a hat with all my years experience spending summers
on burnt-out porches putting together model airplanes
model glue fumes and getting a real kick out of that dude in his
hardhat just hanging on for dear life stuck to a girder in mid-air
without a care just give me some shadowy mildewy basement
all by my lonesome with no one breathing over my shoulder
for purposes of rebirth and redemption with all those cracked
genie bottles to help piece together memories for madmen
who just strayed a little trying to make things right again

The Rituals of Mummification

#39

What did the fog
        & mist
                from the mountain
do to you?
        true-blue
                bell-bottom blues...

didn't you know my heart & soul
was greater than my *good looks*
and just as quick to crumble
from all those crooks willing
to steal it for no rhyme or reason
at the drop of a hat 'cuz they couldn't
have you and i didn't even know that?

how exactly, instinctively,
empirically to measure spirit—

    "we got a hostage situation!"
            & a 6-pack of *schlitz*
                    left for the negotiators

            a final proof:
    didn't have a mean bone
                in my body...

A Hx Of Stream Of Consciousness

#40

Can the heart go abandoned
like a trapdoor to the soul
& mind turned numb
drawing a curtain
on the shattered
snowglobe
losing it all
at the most
inopportune
& profound
of moments?

#41

Whore
bath
reve
lations
like a
lawn
full of
dandy
lions
& vase
of wild
orchids

The Rituals of Mummification

#42

Like the rich
& fertile deep
dark soil farm
land which sir
rounds chicago
going in and out
of it like the run
off from flood
ding of the nile

#43

Like a
reunion
of those
leftover
campers
in those
polaroids
on the
water
skis
in the
human
pyramid

A Hx Of Stream Of Consciousness

#44

Spent a whole season
hanging off a rusty nail
in summer camp but still
managed to sing out—
"you fill up my senses."
when the therapist asked
me my first memories
i told him when they
crumpled up newspapers
and burnt in gigantic
numbers 1970 beneath
the berkshire mountains
am i supposed to feel
something still not sure

#45

When i die don't want
to be dumped in some
old hole in the ground
or my ashes scattered
all around but turned
into chicken mcnuggets
and shared with all those
who once may have cared
or loved me which will be
a party of 3, ballerinas hitching

The Rituals of Mummification

home in the rain; ectasy and xanex
delivered to some insane castle door

#46

How to mow in a hail storm
with your shirt off while
casually smoking a butt
and being well-known
in a small town through
the vfw, barrooms, being
a good son, bad con
and running a number
of the nude watering holes

#47

Drizzle falls on the tall
sheltering pines of fall
right above the donut
shops and bus stops
of some long lost
strange suburb strip
mall where you see
all those cheap movies
just past their release
and your home be
all those welfare
hotels just over

A Hx Of Stream Of Consciousness

the bridge
of cobble
stone of
all those
leftover
forgot
tin
where
you cuddle
with the remains
of the season whispering
sweet nothings whimpering
of foghorns and trainhorns
don't tell me downpour
doesn't have any smell
like putting up scenes
for the holiday season
in department stores

heart & soul calls…

#48

Watching the weather you wish it'd say

feels like rose
feels like seaweed beneath your tired swollen feet
feels like that secret seductive watering hole where
gorgeous high school girls in bikinis with bodies to
die for make it a madonna/whore safe & secure custom

The Rituals of Mummification

to flirt madly with fathers out with their sons making them
feel flattered caught between the fight & flight syndrome
feels like that wild out-of-control highly intelligent passionate
promiscuous borderline girl who helped you explore all parts
of the body & never wanted or for that matter have any desire
to return back to the responsibilities of what hostile life required
feels like a black woman's afro you once loved & never even knew
feels like philadelphia louisiana biloxi butte montana the beautiful
maddening aroma of the mellifluous magnolia grace of gladiolus
ruffled luxuriant petals of pachysandra romance of wild orchid
feels like the wind chimes & chimes of cathedrals
feels like the sun falling in hoboken, nj when you're feeling all alone
in dreary hell's kitchen staring through the keyhole of the skyscrapers
to the hudson river & the only thing holding you together the stray
streaming scents of the season of hotdogshotpretzelshotpeanuts
feels like the paradise & liberation of those mad ghetto citypools on pitt st
& redhook brooklyn with hollering black kids & puerto ricans being completely
anonymous & strangely experiencing the phenomenon of feeling right at home
feels like the heart of the lower east side & sweltering nights picking up plantain
stuffed with chopped meat & that coconut drink coming straight from the machine
feels like the first time you got high on coke heroin & speed & bottles & bottles
of orange *cool breeze* hanging out with ex-cons in tompkins square park
hustling taking shots at *vasack's drinking tavern* & making it with black
girls on harlem rooftops & the next morning feeling on top of the world
taking the subway back at a crawl from 135th to placid palpitating
& palpable brownstone still hungover in carrol gardens brooklyn
feels like a different sort of rolling thunder coming in from the
mountains always providing some kind of rebirth & redemption
feels like what the lonely lascivious midnight lake & lagoon
will do to you wrapped in the holy spirits of croaking

A Hx Of Stream Of Consciousness

bullfrogs the ripple of shore & creaking of docks
feels like the dew of stoops & boardwalks
of wildernesses & ballfields & jungle gyms
& streetcars of bridges & rivers rambling
through villages with the mercurial &
transitory elements sprinkled ephemerally
during the delicate stages of dawn & dusk

#49

Did i happen to mention too
     think they should carve out
  busts for all us long-lost true-blue losers
    on-the-run on the outskirts
  of the long-gone
wailing woebegone
    dakotas
      for all those
also who got abused & alienated
  & taken advantage of
the ones really responsible
  for the building of america
    & just have their bare
broken muscular backs
    turned back
from the whole pack
of awful tourist
of obnoxious asshole
     ugly american

The Rituals of Mummification

looking exactly like
miles davis, jim morrison,
kerouac, howard hughes,
bugsy seagal, lenny bruce
who got put on
the infamous blacklist
for just telling the truth
along with his fellow fore
father jewish comedian
charlie chaplin
literally deported
back to the shores
of merry old england
      & so will literally come upon them
   when you got nothing left to live for
suddenly soaring out
    of the raw landscape & low-lying
            miraculous clouds of montana
after staggering off the greyhound
          methadone
              manifest-destiny
                  bound
      having runaway once again
   as a teenager
underestimated
  being treated no better
        than some poor abused stray dog
            after working one of your
    long impossible graveyards
hustling a yellow

A Hx Of Stream Of Consciousness

        way off on 11th avenue
    as far west as you could get
in misty-eyed manhattan
    where you swear you saw
           strips of snapshot dusk
                night in & night out
    never knowing when it was gonna end
trying to figure it all out
        just as much a slave of the city
            of the madness
        of the seasons
        ghosts mingling
          in boxcar diners
    whores literally taking whore-baths
in opened-up fire hydrants
      of sweltering summer
  these strangers
kindred spirits
    & no doubt feeling just as much a part of it
living some 2nd, 3rd, 4th life & existence
    wouldn't matter if i had lived or died
      like some weatherworn postcard
        with no reply
    those who cast you aside
  were living the lie
while you were dying to live
    like those stray dogs did
      hidden beneath the boardwalk
          in the wicked winter of coney island
                saving up

The Rituals of Mummification

                        enough ends
                    to pawn your tv
                 in the holy snow
            fall
                blizzard
                    of hell's kitchen
                steering your *zenith*
        on luggage wheels
through snowdrifts
                like some russian peasant
    & once again climbing back on
                back once more
                    with the madmen
                        of port authority
        boys escaped from group homes
lowdown criminals
from brokedown hoboken
                    new jersey
                        zooming out to the shores
                                of tenderloin san francisco
in some final
        last-ditch effort to meet up
                    with soulmates
                            not sure if child
        hood best friends, partners, neighbors,
            or having finally discovered
                        they're homosexual
        days seeping into sunsets
into evening
        surviving off spam sandwiches

A Hx Of Stream Of Consciousness

            & mad dog cool breeze 20/20
getting off dazed, ruminating
    somehow feeling redeemed
        in a land where no one
            could possibly know me
    out in sweet lost & lonely
solitary montana
where madmen
& their mamas
tumbleweed
& blustery bison
still wandered the forgotten plains
        swear seeing some strong & handsome
            pure phantom
                not sure whether
                    iroquois? sioux? lakota?
            & in that moment nothing mattered
        pointing his finger towards the horizon
in some longlost lowdown
        blinking blue
            shutdown
                downtown
                    deserttown
                        some endless
                            copper dustyave canyon
        as if just happening to mention
that way, that way
        out to california
            & then resembling something
        of a hobo hero

The Rituals of Mummification

                        disheveled, downtrodden
                            climbing back on
watching it all vanish
    through your desert window…

#50

Remember that whole summer hearing bruce springsteen's
scratchy romantic voice crooning from his masterpiece–
"the river" diving under that deep blue pool not caring
if i ever came up again surviving off bags and bags
from bronx runs of hawaiin gold no one could have
looked more bronzed or handsome showing up
to those barrooms in my blue jeans and brand
new t-shirt and all those older girls older sisters
flirting with me not sure what to do with them
as what dreams were made of and forbidden
returning their seductions with a quick
grin and simply staggering out feeling
flattered which in the moment felt like
only thing in the world that mattered

#51

Radiant, pale, dirty-blonde, angel vagabonds peddle their bicycles
through the mountains and rivers of summer and have the freedom
to actually look up through my window and then disappear through

A Hx Of Stream Of Consciousness

the shadows of the early evening dusk as the geometry of their figures
and form and natural graceful motions in the moment bring back such
keen sentimental memories of my later-adolescent early-adulthood.

you can see from a slight distance they are fragile and romantic
and tempermental almost taking on the selfsame shape of the rivers
and fields and mountains and brilliant maddening change of seasons

holy and sacred stalkers for better or for worse...

#52

She peddles her bicycle
with her blustery sundress
riding up from her bottom
could anything be more
innocent and seductive
dreaming thoughtful
with a basket full of
bouncing apples
and then just
like that like
some transient
phantom vanishes
without cause
or warning
to the clouds
which will
soon be
storming

The Rituals of Mummification

#53

At the tasty cream
     the nurse maid
who's really a witch
whips out her tit
& uses it for a
myriad of reasons
& then simply vanishes
in the chill fall foliage
& skeleton branches
& the wisps of wind
& wail of trainhorns
into the mountains
where all the true
spirits stir swollen
rivers of brilliant
burgeoning silence

#54

Why is it that i still
dream of that red hair
girl with beautiful black
coal eyes tiny breasts
i made it with in that
anonymous motel
somewhere around
midnight on the

A Hx Of Stream Of Consciousness

atlantic ocean
self-soothed by
its silhouettes
and motions
with a muted tv
its only beacon?
is it cuz she just
represented all
pain suffering
and simply
the vague
and opaque
opposite of
everything
and everyone
i have ever
known kept
completely open
ended and without
closure as something
really to be said about
shit like that (like really
getting to know someone
including yourself and the
universe through pillow talk)
with wishes and dreams
and fantasies seeping
through that slightly
open door somewhere
along the coast of maine

The Rituals of Mummification

right around midnight
somewhere around
the atlantic ocean

#55

I'm pretty sure i'm
that film-noir figure
who gets shot up
with bullet holes
through the woe
be gone motel
wall o! holy
and hollow
absolutely
nothing
tragic at all
cause soul
survival
with just
leftover
lingering
light streaming
through anonymous
amorphous darkness
while surrounded
by the natural beauty
of the musicality
of nature and culture

A Hx Of Stream Of Consciousness

and a view of the brilliant
vacant void of nothingness
the lakes and rivers swollen over
and the cattle never brought in during
thundering downpour while just don't feel
anything at all being instantly forgotten
as upon introspection and self-reflection
my belief of a certain sort of forgiveness

#56

Are some good small towns out here
where that nurse who takes my blood
pressure and soul also mows the lawns
of all the parks and graveyards and think
deep down inside dudes really want some
girl who will take control and holler out through
the home–"honey i'm going out to mow!" bringing
back real down home ghost stories maybe even
a six as you stagger home through the dazzling
discerning dusk with all hope restored or at least
no more on-the-run through all those gorgeous
wild hypnotizing girls in cut-off shorts starting
all that murder and mayhem and taking
boys even the young men hostage in
mind body and spirit knowing exactly
what they are doing; families returning
home like a blissful juggernaut and exodus
along the side of the road with all the world

The Rituals of Mummification

off their shoulders from minor league baseball
looking as if they have had their hearts and
souls saved or maybe possibly worries
slightly delayed in abeyance as you get
swept up by the miraculous delicious
scents from backyard barbecues and
swirling chimneys following their tempting
trail through the monstrous sunflowers and
community gardens and drive-ins and pools
and pristine courthouses and burnt-down
haunted houses a new and improved man
or rather former shell of yourself which
strangely enough feels far more real

#57

It's strange, my tv gives me
the weather in the holy land
of israel and disney world
but not where i live in the
mountains of vermont
yet don't really care
so much so long
as i got that saint
and seductress
maria delerosa
her hot italian
rubenesque
hourglass

A Hx Of Stream Of Consciousness

figure
sweeping
across the
heartland
and dust
bowl
of my
melon
cholia

#58

Back in new york city we used to stick our heads
in the freezer during the sweltering summer to cool
down a little. i was thinking just recently with all this
global warming might just stick my whole body in there
and just sit in there like "the thinker" minding my own
business and figure out all my issues and conflicts; wife
oblivious poking around for chicken fingers and fish sticks

#59

Seeping paint
pouring rain
that be me
on a bleak day
in an impress
mystic painting
trying to find

The Rituals of Mummification

my way
in turn of
the century
vienna, new
york city–
"anybody
know a place
to get good
chinese?"
all irrelevant
as all about
getting lost
& trying to
find your way
back home
in ole time
cosa-nostra
cobblestone

#60

Having terrible dreams
not being able to sleep
i sleepwalk down the hall
to the living room with the tv still on
and keep it on for these exact reasons
and it was the comedian don rickles with that
eternal pasted-on smirk dressed like a prisoner
with maxwell smart and he was just rubbing

A Hx Of Stream Of Consciousness

his head and belly which caused me to crack
up and just couldn't stop laughing and forgot
what enzyme and gland that was but caused
me to go to bed a really happy man with
some real silly and stupid grin and looking
back at my existence it was people like this;
get smart, wonder woman, batman & robin
who always just helped me to forget (which
i think is saying something) far more than i can
say about most humans i ever met; a slapstick comedian
and straight man just sitting there face to face very sincere
and earnest, poised and pathetic, like buddha casting
off his enemies fading away in the cone of silence

in the morning wake up to a muted lucy & ricky bickering

#61

I haven't changed; just all them who betrayed
sometimes you got to dig deep into the shallows

#62

A prickly poisonous rose
blooms past my window
she grew up in the boroughs
and almost like some daily
tradition or ethnic-cleansing
will threaten to stab me

The Rituals of Mummification

on a daily basis makes
me feel more a part of
things and a connection
while her mom who hates
men for good reason
as religiously cheated
on by an ex-husband
who was a banker
and ended up marrying
the last chick he was with
and upgraded himself from
a reform jew to a conservative
and the wife and her joke with
each other upon one of her visits
that i was abducted of which i am
sympathetic and seems pretty accurate

#63

I see a stickie stuck on our
kitchen counter "call jesus."
i call out– "i'm gonna kill
you tom sawyer!" fooling
around with my kid as like
to torture him a bit; how we
show our affection taking after
injun joe, television-version chasing tom
and becky thatcher through the darkness
of the caves. my kid ignores me having

A Hx Of Stream Of Consciousness

gotten used to it just the way i like it
and digs into his *hardy boys* while
moon comes up over the mountain

#64

We finally made it up here
like the von traps escaping
nazi-occupied austria up in
to the breathtaking swiss alps
with a droopy wild apple tree
dropping apples into our yard
during the heat; the only thing
that really makes any sense
to me or makes me feel worthy
the winos come out in the season
adding character to the neighbor
hood and a fog which slips down
the mountain around the mounds
of silhouetted matchstick steeples

#65

Horses transported
through torrents of rain
in the change of seasons
from the dusk to evening

Coming up: weather
              ghosts

The Rituals of Mummification

#66

Why i want someone like buster keaton for prez
half-crazed, athletic, malleable, all-weathered
with the melodramatic wind constantly blowing
through his hair on some runaway train, plane
or ship, well-equipped 'cause always in crisis
or the punch line to that quip 'trouble always
seems to find me,' finding ingenious and easy
ways out of it due to repetition and experience
holding on for dear life, always seeming to get
the pretty girl in the end, all heroic and slapstick
as i feel absolutely nothing for our new old batch
of candidates who are supposedly supposed to
represent our best interests, but got no idea and
just don't feel it and feel like i been through this
type of shit before, and back then *trust* me wasn't
impressed; perhaps even get his stepbrother w.c.
fields to be speaker of the house, literally nodding-
out beneath derby hat, strawberry-nosed, bloated,
blush-faced, dozing off off a jug of moonshine
with one of those long hilarious tremendous
harmonizing three stooges' snores which
always seemed to say it all; his stud-gigolo
cousin infamous, self-destructive, deathwish
d.w. griffith for vice president, spinning on the top
of his head slipping and sliding somewhere between
stoic and sympathetic on some 76th fl. ledge on top of some
turn of the century black and white skyscraper looking down
on all of humanity really knowing it all, quick and clever

A Hx Of Stream Of Consciousness

hustler, while ironically feel so much more comfortable
and better represented, muted, and with the sound off

#67

Batman gets up in robin
for once again forgetting
the suction cups and rope
and being a fuck-up and tells
him when they get back to the
wayne manor oi gavalt! gonna
make him climb the batpole ten
times in a row; jots a letter to riddler
and rolls a blunt; what's with all this
fucken global warming i'm schvitzing!

#68

i want them to show up as well
for all things petty & trivial
i want them to lay out the liars
i want them to beat down betrayal
i want them to combat the politicians
as soulless & phony as sibling rivalry
i want them to strangle, mafia-style
all those who start kvetching
& thrive off the gossip & rumor
i want them to slow dance with all those
who feel unduly deserted & abandoned

The Rituals of Mummification

with all hearts sounding like a ticking
time bomb until it all settles to a calm
like some self-soothing river of the mind
i want them to swing over every bridge
& smooch every statue & bastion
begging for forgiveness & redemption
i want them to sit shiva on orchard &
nod-out on hudson river crossings
waking up after having passed-out
on the counter at that diner in hoboken
over their stuffed derma & cup of coffee
i want them to become charter members
of alcoholic's anonymous & methadone clinics
when their psychiatrists suggest their losing it
i want them to steal back their identities
that got ripped-off so suddenly by the rich
kids from the suburbs with connections &
nepotism & privilege & entitlement, put a patent on it
self-advocated & turned themselves into arrogant ass
hole self-promoting modern-day heroes & heroines
i want to see them all wrapped up in that human
knot in the back of the crosstown bus when
they feel like they're losing touch, got no
one to turn to & nothing left to live for
i want them to wake up the bum
& return him back home
i want them to revive the wino
& give him a new title
i want to see them schmooze
with old black men who now

A Hx Of Stream Of Consciousness

live in the park & used to be
artists & gave up on it all after
got played-out by white girls
who they thought loved them
i want them to threaten
the superintendent
& lynch the landlord
& send them to their
final resting place
where they belong
i want them to have revelations
or at least a reason for living
a sense of belonging, being
& believing under the rhythm
& beat of the beat barreling el
i want them to get rid of all skeletons
& pick up the pretty girls at the riverdale
diner around the reservoir on jerome avenue
in the boogie-down bronx after getting drunk,
breaking habits, developing new ones, having
rebirths & gaining a whole new perspective
i want them to bang on the billboard removing
histrionics from the expressions and the happily
ever after which never ever quite seems to happen
& suddenly feel real again not falling for
the schtick sex appeal see-through spiel
i want to see them on the side of a milk
carton breakfast of champions little dab
will do you bunnyhop dance step manual
i want them to sneak through the trap

The Rituals of Mummification

door of the flesh & folds of the
haunted & holy heart & soul
i want to see them show up just after
a drug dealer gets stabbed in the park
& ambulance drivers spar & get
involved in a power struggle about
which hospital will take him due to
insurance & the next day finding out
he perished from the newspapers of old
men on benches & the homeless hotelier
who all vanished as well down delancey
to the holy hallelujah swells of the east river
i want to see them scoot up the fire escape
back to where they belong while up on top
that lower east side rooftop everything
lost comes back in the sacred moment
of chinatown good ol' shanghai joe's
midnight prowling at katz's, ratner's
& kosar's bialy's opening up
right before the dawn sweeping
the kosher flour from the floor
bookstores they used to slave
in all day all night long in soho
that stray cat taking a cat nap
on top the garbage can in the
warm winter sun of brooklyn
i want to see them meet up with
joe buck & ratso rizzo & give them
some reason 'to keep on keeping on'
i want them to sweep through the seasons

A Hx Of Stream Of Consciousness

& bleary-eyed, bummed, sincerely become
one with the bleak neon streets which
splendidly sink into the valley & alleys
of the streaming swarms of humanity
i want them to worship every evening
that gorgeous girl in publishing
who shows up to her window
like some miraculous beacon
unbeknownst, innocent, bare-
boned, naked, like some edward
hopper portrait, like some sexy
savior from the cornfields
overlooking all lost souls
& rises & is as alive as
the glowing moon & sun
i want to see them decked-
out in drag like cross-dressing
detectives keeping an eye out
on the higher-than-holy hasidim
in the midnight meat market
looking to get blown by the
drag queens when things
aren't going quite right
in their marriages
i want to see them save felix unger
for the millioneth time after he threatens
to kill himself when his wife 'requests that
he leaves his place of residence' & now takes
residence with the pigeons with his back pasted
up against the summer brick hysterical flailing

The Rituals of Mummification

trembling petrified with a panoramic view
of central park where they used to show
commercials for seedy tourist hotels
right in the heart of times square
where the hustlers & petty thieves
& drug dealers used to turn your
dreams to nightmares in some cruel
& brutal real life game of truth or dare
i want them to be drowned-out
by the calling-out of that devout
diva to die for in her hysterical holy
hypnotic soprano of "taa-axi!" while
they literally grind to a screeching
halt outside the polish diners on
avenue a of tompkin's square park
where hendrix used to jam all day long
& the black panthers rumbled the hell's
angels as each one goes flying into their
respective cab & takes off in a plume
of dust to the upper west side where
the jewish scholar, blacklisted
intellectual, out-of-work actor
& tal's bagels got their start
i want to see them climbing
up the side of brick edifices
while they do close-ups of
them chit-chatting, rapping
& tugging at that infamous rope
up bankrupt woolworth's, harcourt-
brace, citi-corp, the flat iron & empire

A Hx Of Stream Of Consciousness

state building which they can never
take down even if they dreamed
spiritually, historically, aesthetically
& encompasses all of our memories
consciousness of being & civilization
i want to see them somersaulting from
the skull from the heart & soul from
the doll's head from the bat signal
from the blinking beacon full moon
swooning beaming over the brooklyn
bridge to tombs in downtown manhattan
where they keep the delinquents hidden
ready to get shipped to rykers island based
on mistaken identity & guilt by association
i want to see them show up to family
get-togethers & sock square in the jaw
all those who oversaw pain & damage
with those cartoon bubbles of "powww!"
"swaack!" & "kerplunk!" then just take-off
with doggie bags of cold cuts & ambrosia
i want to see them passed-out
drunken & disheveled still in
their cape crusader crime-fighting
costumes surrounded by stiff business
men oblivious snapping their papers heading
home on the metro north back to the suburbs
i want them to mess-up the mean-spirited
like those gorgeous puerto rican girls
rubbing garlic on their fingernails
& scratching rivals eyes out

The Rituals of Mummification

how did that song go again?
"all by myself..." as all life
tippy-toes through the keyhole
& you were always able to come
up with some punchline while still
down-in-the-dumps & suffered
as such a fine line between
slapstick & crises & could
faintly hear the bells from the
cathedral bounce & resound
off the cobblestone going
"bong! bong! bong! bong!"
which somehow seemed
to count down your mortality
& profoundly exacerbate your
solitary loneliness in this thing
called living & would instantly
assuage & make you feel
strangely alive while
at the same time brings
out all the stray dogs
from right beneath
the peanut brittle brine
of the hushabye boardwalk
i want batman & robin
to be found coughing
like steve austin
man barely alive
in the phone booth
tonto on unemployment

A Hx Of Stream Of Consciousness

c chaplin deported
   & toot shores slipping
      out the steamy doors
           of the automat
               after a revolving
hot plate feast
      of kielbasa
          & stuffed cabbage

#69

Reality show stars
doing commercials for aspirin
#1 neurologist recommended…

every summer someone's
gotta do something really stupid
at *walmart* to get famous like warhol in vegas

#70

Back in the day all those ancient egyptians
got buried with their best friend companions
so they'd remain with them till the bitter end

what the hell? would people now ask
to get buried with their i-phones (fuck you
all!) to know snow still melts from the pinnacle

The Rituals of Mummification

of the himalayas and flows all the way down
to help the ganges go; wasn't that the river
kept you young or helped just to forget it all?

"Where have you gone Joe Dimaggio
a nation turns its lonely eyes to you…"

#71

When joe d was tearing through his streak
the statistician who stood inside "the green
monster" at fenway would feed ted williams
his rival in center field a swing-by-swing
at-bat account through a hole in the fence
who in turn passed on the information to his
brother dom who i believed played left for the sox

things like that don 't happen too often anymore…

#72

Childhood used to have this dream
of wandering through this empty
mall and getting that poster of daryl
dawkins "chocolate thunder" sitting
on his throne, but probably wouldn't
fit as being a new yorker walls already
clogged with walt "clyde" frazier, bob mcadoo,
earl "the pearl" monroe; getting older, remember
older sister giggling with her girlfriends noticing

A Hx Of Stream Of Consciousness

the sudden change and phases to my walls with
glossy cut-outs of brooke shields and cheryl tiegs
in that fishnet bikini not leaving a whole hell
of a lot of room open for the imagination

what dreams were made of...

#73

Weren't those keenest memories and days
dusk games we used to play after supper
with lingering scents and aromas still
swirling around the kitchen straying
down halls and foyers like some
hypnotic halo and getting the rest
of your insane mad energy out with
kids from the neighborhood until against
your own will and volition with a realistic
tragic amount of resistance had to drag
your action & adventure black & blue
bones back in to bathe the rest of the earth
and lay of the land away and hit the sheets
and dream innocently, intensely, about your
future with a slight twinkle of moon like some
eternal beacon sneaking through bedroom curtains?

#74

See where some scientists from
down on earth are getting a little

The Rituals of Mummification

freaked-out by some image they
think they see on the red planet
of some tall skinny girl with long
hair they believe might be living
up there alone and i think wow
pretty damn cool and have a
trigger of old girlfriends i once
loved and what happened to them
and leave her the fuck alone as good
to know there's some tall skinny girl
with long hair up there keeping an eye
out for all us poor lost souls from above

#75

Little boy blue
behind the blinds
hiding on the moon
wanted, never the right
kind more dead than alive

#76

There should be some kind
of super syrup elixir medicine
for diarrhea or heartburn or indigestion
or something to finally soothe & heal
the internal organs & all the bullshit
& brainwash of american exceptionalism

A Hx Of Stream Of Consciousness

& just sit back lazy like like a real life
solitary nietzchian archie bunker in
your easy chair & swig it & helps to
pretend like none of this ever existed

#77

Somehow i'm more sympathetic
(even got more respect) when they
speak of our opiate problem and just
like america got the need and compulsion
to 'break it all down' state by state like the
wealthiest man in the world or best colleges

#78

Why not when the presidential candidates
choose their vp running mates one of them
takes a full-fledged risk & throws their hat
in the ring & picks a madame or dominatrix
equipped with her leather mask & uniform &
zippers & whip standing by their side all silent
& stoic & would provide them the necessary
discipline when needed if their heads get too
big or need to keep them in check & things in
perpective; the only conflict if perhaps one
of them bites the dust or gets sick, how she
will translate to domestic & foreign affairs?

The Rituals of Mummification

#79

Usually some time in the wee hours of the night
after crashing and waking up from my easy chair
i make sure to put on the weather channel for the
following morning as it might just straight-up
show scenes from nebraska; if i get lucky
fargo, north dakota and pick me up a little
and start to inch my way around the home

#80

I can barely get through the night with all my nightmares
and wonder why the hell they won't even leave me alone
in here? i wake up to a wife pissed-off and hostile for what?
what? wanting to make the relationship a little bit better?
more romantic and affectionate and intimate? more
soothing to the touch? and somehow convince
myself to get out of bed to a not very convincing
existence and even wonder what *this* all represents?

i look back with fondness to a life of one-night stands…

#81

Getting lost is the best way in
finding what you're really looking for

A Hx Of Stream Of Consciousness

matter of fact the damaged heart & soul paradoxically
even becomes more receptive and porous like osmosis
taking in emotion, compassion, knowledge and wisdom

#82

I was recently ruminating about what it would be like
for someone with severe and profound tourette's
on their deathbed, while think it might just be
so much more (sur)real than all that other bullshit
power-struggle of family posturing and wrangling
and aligning and ceremony and believe in my
opinion would hold so much more meaning
going off with a couple last sleazy words

a commercial for a blooming onion
a butterfly floating in from the woods…

#83

Has anyone ever called up their beloved barber
to make an appointment 'cuz knew the following
day they'd be on-the-run from the fuzz who always
manage to find nothing or someone just as alone
as you literally end up rapping back and forth
about stuff and in the end he even asks if
there are any positions open in your field

know that clichéd expression
about making a difference?

The Rituals of Mummification

#84

You sit at the diner
all day brooding in desolation
downing cup after cup of coffee

you ask if they accept personal checks…

#85

Told me i had that look
on my face like the day
she tried to commit suicide
and didn't want to leave me
that night; never crossed my
mind but thought a fine
and sweet gesture and
why the hell not
could really use
the company…

#86

The intricate
& delicate tendrils
of that kaleidoscopic
spider web which
magically materializes
& gets put up night in

A Hx Of Stream Of Consciousness

& night out by the secret
elements & wonders of
the sandman majestically
hanging from a pine branch
outside your window right
in front of the mountain
then naturally vanishes
from the rays of the sun

#87

6 o'
clock
in the
morning
through
the dusty
blinds of
melon
collie
bed
room
in the
day
luge
of the
meow
tins
of my

The Rituals of Mummification

back
yard
sea
alone
deer
just
minding
his own
snout
pressed
up against
the damp
drenched
forest
leaves
scav
ging
allows
me to
get a
little
taste
of reality
to finally
get up
like dracula
with a hang
over forget
ting thank
fully what

went down
the night
before

#88

Yellow finch
please don't
ditch the wire
from dusk
until night
(i need you
by my side)
until your
heart's
desire
until
i feel
right

#89

Best time
for nap
time
when
the heat
breaks
& sky

The Rituals of Mummification

finally
breaks
open
for kids
& old
men
alike

#90

Planting blue tulips in the red sky
beside the deep green lake hoping they'll
spring up next year right around the apocalypse

that the rabbits won't steal them
like the crows took our
dwarf watermelons

#91

Dew from the mountain
sprinkles husks of corn
like the tears of jesus
looking to be reborn

A Hx Of Stream Of Consciousness

#92

Wild turkey mother
teaching her newborn
to waddle then heading
in alphabetical order
back up the mountain

#93

The workaholic
woodpecker
hammering
on barn
during
the dregs
of summer
an ect of the soul
and down in the
dump doldrums
making me feel
alive once more

#94

Rooster howls like a madman on top of the plateau
but not really mad at all yet purely primal and gotta
get it all out which instinctively get and don't even
think about it if you ever really stop to think about it

The Rituals of Mummification

#95

He sounds no different than brando
hollering–"stell-lla!" or james dean
declaring–"you're tearing me ap-part!"

like some sudden spontaneous slapstick
punchline without the need for the build-
up of that long-winded complicated riddle

#96

And so when it all goes to rot and all the punks
crawl out from under their rocks and have had
enough all you can do is call out your kid and
tell him to lay out and bring out his colored
pencils and crayons and coloring books
(the eternal connect-the-dots to the infinite
transcendent soul) color his books book
his colors cook his brothers in the driving
rain whip out and dump out all the jigsaw
puzzles all over the floor the unimaginable
hot air balloons barns and covered bridges
while dear please i respectfully demand you
strap me down and shoot me up with the drug
of the day hear opiates ain't bad won't even hide
it under my tongue dope! heroin! opium! done it all
actually lying haven't done the last one the last one
lying there like some sulking sunflower in his easy
chair rain coming down in droves drove to wichita

A Hx Of Stream Of Consciousness

kansas the dakotas butte montana met more in the
bleary-eyed biscuit & gravy boxcar diners all by
my lonesome and learned more than you could
ever begin to imagine if you don't mind me saying
will pick up the kid and his mad mischievous pals
after school tomorrow and escape to the mountains
as know all the bridges to jump off of the rivers and
wild waterfalls the secret watering holes tie up my
high top sneakers and jump right in and come back
free men free man buddha got in all those buddha
lotus style positions not necessarily because he was
being one or numb or holy and sacred but as a form
of escapism and just couldn't take it and just didn't
want to be bothered by the outside world anymore
and the wife being a nudge and how they drain you
trust me with that great big wraparound grin pained
expression like kurt cobain when they wouldn't stop
hassling him jim morrison teeny-boppers knocking
on knocking down jean kerouac's cabin door trying
to steal his manuscripts and just one more morsel
of his weatherworn soul tomorrow am going on an
interview to be a "life enrichment counselor" can
you imagine and so damn perverse and ironic cuz
always something i'm so much more desperate for
and in need of like some solitary secluded soul rocking
back and forth on his rocking horse stranded in front
of the window during the change of seasons when
the oil trucks and chopped wood trucks and school
buses stuffed with children from the lagoon suddenly
show up out of nowhere probably see those old timers

The Rituals of Mummification

i'm working with leaping out the courtroom window
like injun jim on-the-run in that episode of tom sawyer

#97

Bill the kid was just trying to make it and make a name for himself
completely misunderstood and underestimated one of the biggest
romantics coming from unfortunate circumstances and wanted to
merely be included and considered a member of the quote on quote
community as they got no idea what it feels like to be alienated
to be stigmatized and criminalized and if only these fake tourists
and ostracizing and mean-spirited churchgoers knew deep down
inside who the true criminals were, like might he once be invited
to some square dance some pig roast some watering hole open up
his own private thriving business of granite to carve out tombstones
and make a name for himself and watch the angels dance with the
ghosts even settle for being a part of some construction crew who
ironically were so much more spoiled and aloof looking down
at their cell phones in front of the chinese buffet and settles
instead for taking a nice long drag in his soiled rags in front
of the old psychiatric institute hoping to get picked up like
some prostitute coming out in the light after a long night
in the town jail by someone who's just as lonely and suffers
just as much some older distinguished woman who might really
appreciate and get him for what he is and what they're not and
ain't that what it's all really about and would just chop down trees
into logs mowing the lawn humming the beasties 'looking down
the barrel of a gun' something not just the cosa-nostra but also
the irish mob and puerto ricans and brothers loved as she

A Hx Of Stream Of Consciousness

would bathe and feed him making small talk while picking
up his wine at *walmart* and dreaming of that very pleasant
radiant and modest and humble mexican girl pushing his
child up the hill in the drizzle with just a small little cabin
chimney smoke coming out of it set back in the mountains

#98

I don't ever want to be
come famous must be
like one of those cliche
punch lines inside a
fortune cookie rather
be one of those sketchy
portraits on a packet
of sugar like one of
those presidents
nobody knows
who knows who be
rutherford b hayes
first one who got
assassinated for
got his name
the one who
came before
lincoln while
all my facts
add up to
absolutely

The Rituals of Mummification

nothing
(my birth
place: long
island jewish
having dropped
out of school to
pursue a career
in wandering)
pouring me
onto some
thing
some
perfectly
stiff
silent
sibling
from thee
obscenely
wealthy suburbs
or taboo romantic
lovers & mistresses
hollow, desperate
making a go at it
in some quaint
& cheap secret
bed & breakfast
on the outskirts
of reality just
to make their
miserable lives

A Hx Of Stream Of Consciousness

& existential
crises seem
just a little bit
better & can
breathe again
give me sum
meaning sprinkling
me all over some
tea & crumpets
torn & crumpled
in the mourn
full morning
hung over
hung over
some sea
somewhere
between
the beat
& rhythm
of the build
up of great
big slow
silent
suspense
full half
crazed
waves
eventually
raucously
creeping

The Rituals of Mummification

& crashing
like cymbals
finding
their way
after their
great myth
logical
journey
onto shore
with some
long deep
shallow roar
then that drawl
when it slips
slowly off
back to where
it came from
waiting for it
to repeat the same
melody the only
thing which seems
to really make any
sense to me or
for that matter
save me
all a part
of the same
bleak brilliant
symphony
where no

A Hx Of Stream Of Consciousness

body knows
me leaving me
empty all i really
ever wanted to be

#99

A strange obscure shipwreck of criminals and comedians
capsized in the cornfield with a haunted sweeping wind
through the weeping willow that will measure out what the
years did to you or all of those fears you can no longer feel

#100

That girl who lived on the lush lawn next door
in that split-level right over some split-rail fence
who felt the need to show me hers under the porch
strangely enough felt like that empty feeling you
get after getting flattered and not knowing what
you did to deserve it as shuffled home confused
and conflicted like after some breakup or slut who
told me she had a crush or declared her love for me

The Rituals of Mummification

#101

All those
weird
creepy
elements
of child
hood
you
some
how
in the
here
&
now
find
your
self sim
pathetic
to & can
relate to
as true
blue just
trying to
find ways
of getting by

as we're all
just really
leftover
ghosts
on the sly
hung out
to dry.

The Rituals of Mummification

About the Author

Joseph Reich is a social worker and displaced New Yorker who lives with his wife and eleven-year-old son up in the high mountains of Vermont. He has been published in a wide variety of eclectic literary journals both here and abroad, and been nominated six times for The Pushcart Prize.

Other Books by Joseph D. Reich

A Different Sort Of Distance (Skive Magazine Press, 2010)
If I Told You To Jump Off The Brooklyn Bridge (Flutter Press, 2010)
Pain Diary: Working Methadone & The Life & Times Of The Man Sawed In Half
    (Brick Road Poetry Press, 2010)
Drugstore Sushi (Thunderclap Press, 2010)
Escaping Shangrila (Punkin Press, 2011)
The Derivation of Cowboys and Indians (Fomite Press, 2012)
The Housing Market: a comfortable place to jump off the end of the world
    (Fomite Press, 2013)
The Hole That Runs Through Utopia (Fomite Press, 2014)
Taking The Fifth And Running With It: A Psychological Guide for the Hard of Hearing
    and Blind (Broadstone Books, 2015)
Connecting the Dots to Shangrila: A Postmodern Cultural History of America
    (Fomite Press, 2016)

Selected Books from Sagging Meniscus Press

Aaron Anstett *Moreover*

Wheeler Antabanez *The Old Asylum and Other Stories*

Laura Davenport *An Occasional History*

Jack Foley *The Tiger and Other Tales*; *Grief Songs*

Matthew Gasda *Orchid Elegy*

Tyler Gore *My Life of Crime*

Charles Holdefer *Dick Cheney in Shorts*

Alvin Krinst *The Yalta Stunts*

Roy Lisker *In Memoriam Einstein*; *Lincoln Center in July and Other Stories*

J.F. Mamjjasond & Fafnir Finkelmeyer *Hoptime*

Stephen Moles *The Most Wretched Thing Imaginable*

M.J. Nicholls *The House of Writers*; *The Quiddity of Delusion*

Joseph D. Reich *The Rituals of Mummification*

Christopher Carter Sanderson *The Too-Brief Chronicle of Judah Lowe*

Jacob Smullyan *Dribble*; *Errata*

Raymond M. Smullyan *A Mixed Bag: Jokes, Puzzles, Riddles and Memorabilia*

John Tynan *Voice Lessons and Other Poems*

Fay Webern *The Button Thief of East Fourteenth Street*